Passengers Once More

New and reopened stations and lines since 1948

SCOTLAND

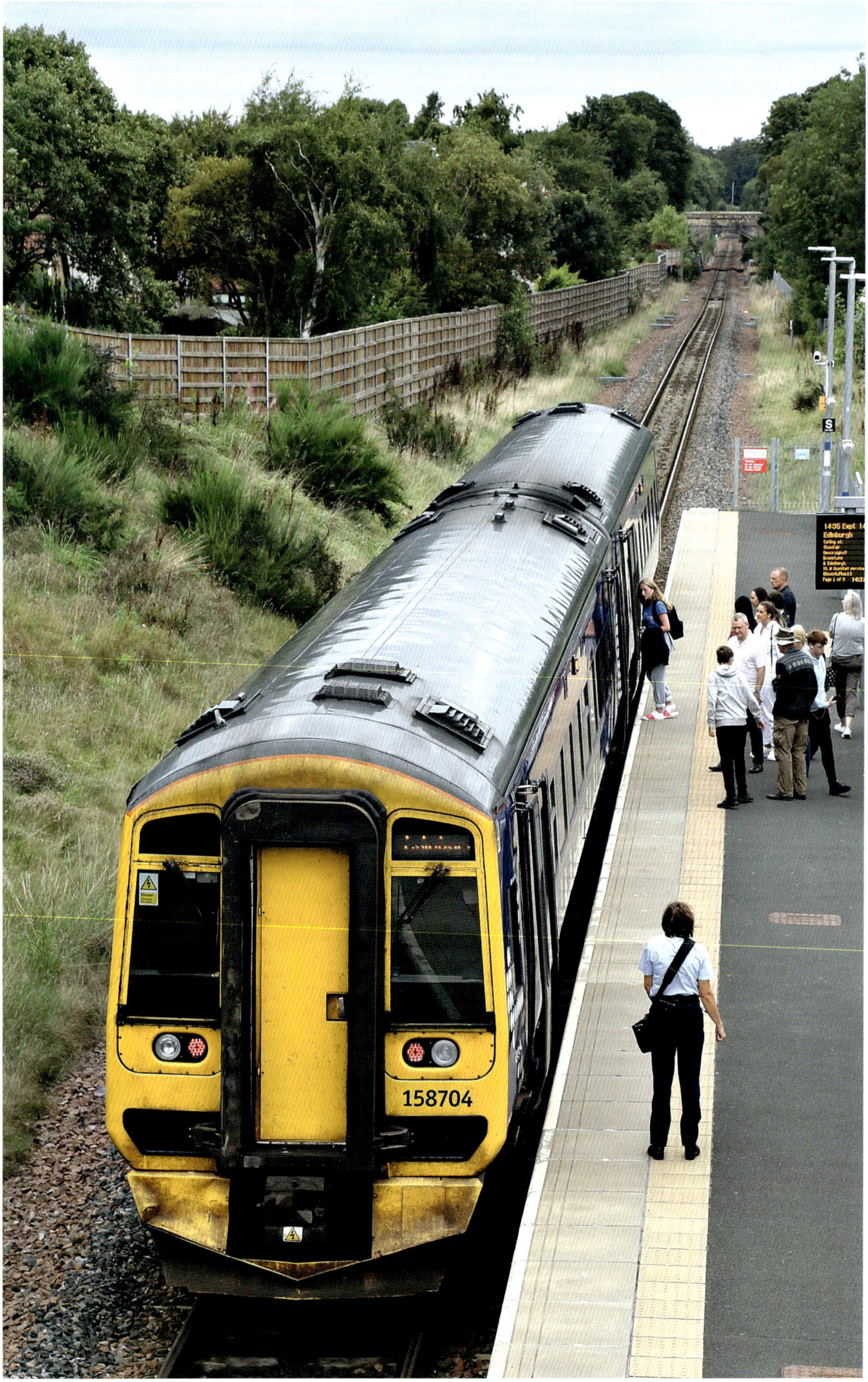
158704
Edinburgh

Passengers Once More

New and reopened stations and lines since 1948

SCOTLAND

Bob Avery and Terry Gough ARPS

SLP

Silver Link Books

© Bob Avery and Terry Gough 2021

All rights reserved. No part of this publication may be reproduced, stored in a retrieval system or transmitted, in any form or by any means, electronic, mechanical, photocopying, recording or otherwise, without prior permission in writing from Silver Link Books, Mortons Media Group Ltd.

First published in 2021

British Library Cataloguing in Publication Data

A catalogue record for this book is available from the British Library.

ISBN 978 1 85794 557 7

Silver Link Books
Mortons Media Group Limited
Media Centre
Morton Way
Horncastle
LN9 6JR
Tel/Fax: 01507 529535

email: sohara@mortons.co.uk
Website: www.nostalgiacollection.com

Printed and bound in the Czech Republic

PLEASE NOTE that details of train services given in this book reflect the situation prior to temporary timetables on many lines due to the COVID situation. Always check with the operator before travelling.

Abbreviations

B&KR	Bo'ness & Kinneil Railway	HR	Highland Railway
BR	British Railways	HST	High Speed Train
CR	Caledonian Railway	LNER	London & North Eastern Railway
DMU	Diesel multiple unit	NBR	North British Railway
ECML	East Coast Main Line	NR	Network Rail
EMU	Electric multiple unit	SRPS	Scottish Railway Preservation Society
G&SWR	Glasgow & South Western Railway	tpd	trains per day
GB&KR	Glasgow, Barrhead & Kilmarnock Railway	TPE	TransPennine Express
		tph	trains per hour
GNSR	Great North of Scotland Railway	WCML	West Coast Main Line
GWR	Great Western Railway	WD	War Department

Frontispiece: The 14.00 Tweedbank-Edinburgh service makes its call at Eskbank on 14 August 2019. *Bob Avery*

Right: The site of the new station at Inverness Airport, looking east on 16 August 2019. *Bob Avery*

Contents

Introduction and acknowledgements	6
Highland stations	9
Strathspey Railway	19
Morayshire stations (Keith & Dufftown Railway)	23
Aberdeenshire stations	27
Royal Deeside Railway	32
Angus stations (Caledonian Railway (Brechin) Ltd)	33
Tayside stations	36
Fife stations	40
Perth to Ladybank line	44
Stirling area stations	45
Argyll/Lochaber (West Highland Lines)	48
Edinburgh and Lothians	51
Edinburgh to Airdrie via Bathgate	51
The Borders Railway	59
Other Edinburgh and Lothians stations	67
Winchburgh Junction to Dalmeny Junction line	76
Bo'ness & Kinneil Railway	76
Greater Glasgow stations	80
Argyle Line	80
Paisley Canal line	86
Rutherglen East Junction to Whifflet	90
Glasgow Queen Street to Anniesland	94
Larkhall line	98
Other Greater Glasgow stations	101
Greater Glasgow lines	118
Ayrshire stations	120
Barassie to Kilmarnock line	125
Dumfries & Galloway stations	126
Index of locations	128

Introduction and acknowledgements

Welcome to this, the final volume in Silver Link's 'Passengers Once More' series.

Few would disagree that the Scottish Government, with powers vested in it by the Railways Act of 2005, has shown the rest of the UK how it's done when it comes to the reopening of stations and lines and the development of new rail services. A string of major reopenings – some from well before 2005 – illustrate the point. Glasgow's subterranean Argyle Line, lines from Rutherglen to Whifflet, from Edinburgh to Glasgow via Bathgate and Airdrie, from Hamilton to Larkhall, and of course the Borders Railway are major achievements indeed. All have exceeded projected usage, in some cases by considerable margins.

In addition to these major schemes, numerous other stations have been built as completely new, or are resurrections of those long closed, and more are in the pipeline.

It seems that in Scotland the powers that be realise that public transport must provide a practical alternative to the car, train frequencies must avoid long waits where possible, and connections must be straightforward. By and large the projects mentioned have been successful in achieving these ideals. In my own home town in Lanarkshire, the local rail service to Glasgow now starts earlier, finishes later, has doubled in frequency (before the Covid-19 pandemic of 2020-21), runs on Sundays and offers many more journey opportunities than it did when I moved here 35 years ago – not to mention several through trains each day to Edinburgh and Ayr. And car parking has been drastically improved.

Most stations have 24-hour CCTV screening. This has improved security on stations and generally they are no longer frightening places in which to wait after dark, and are largely (but not entirely) free of vandalism and graffiti.

Of course, nothing's perfect. Many stations have limited services in the evenings, and it still seems to be a presumption in high places that few people want to go anywhere on Sundays, even though Scotland is free of the shopping hours restrictions that exist south of the border. Many local bus services stop around 7pm. Although car parks at stations are generally free of charge and covered by CCTV surveillance, some stations have inadequate parking facilities or none at all. And ScotRail's current franchise holder has had a crisis period recently with train crew shortages brought about by a number of factors, resulting in higher than acceptable levels of cancellations and resultant bad press.

But these are temporary problems and will no doubt be overcome in time. The list of ongoing initiatives continues, and is not limited to the central belt. The Aberdeen to Inverness line is the recipient of a rolling programme of investment with the aim of providing an hourly service, a reduction in journey time and an increase in passengers commuting by rail into the cities at either end, as well as new stations at Dalcross (Inverness Airport – construction yet to start) and Kintore (near Aberdeen – now open). Tied in with this is the Aberdeen Crossrail project – where trains will run from Inverurie through Aberdeen towards Stonehaven and Montrose and beyond to the south. And as this volume closes for press, news is breaking of the Scottish Government's approval for the next stage in the process of reinstatement of part of the former branch from Thornton Junction to Methil in Fife, to serve Cameron Bridge and Leven. Reopening is currently estimated for five years hence. In addition, recent press reports suggest a possibility of a new West Highland Line station to serve the military port of Faslane.

In the Western Highlands, services between Glasgow and Oban have been doubled from three to six per day (except Sundays). In the Lothians, Transport Scotland has committed to deliver new stations at Reston and East Linton on the East Coast Main Line (ECML) between Edinburgh and Berwick. The service is likely to be an extension of the current ScotRail service from Edinburgh to Dunbar (which has acquired a second platform).

In the densely populated Central Belt there are now no fewer than five fully electrified routes between Edinburgh and Glasgow. Listing from the north, they are:

- a half-hourly service from Glasgow Queen Street via Springburn, Cumbernauld and Falkirk Grahamston (now also calling at the

Introduction and acknowledgements

new Robroyston station in Glasgow's eastern suburbs)
- a 15-minute-interval 'fast' service from Queen Street via Falkirk High, Croy, Polmont and Linlithgow
- a 15-minute-interval service via Airdrie and Bathgate (alternating stopping/semi-fast service)
- a half-hourly service (again alternating stopping/semi-fast) from Glasgow Central via Shotts
- a limited service from Glasgow Central via Motherwell and Carstairs, with some services extending to Ayr in the west and North Berwick in the east.

All these services run to Edinburgh Waverley and also call at Haymarket. Edinburgh has of course also gained a light rail system – currently being extended – though this is outwith the scope of this book.

Elsewhere in Scotland a number of projects are receiving serious consideration. The extension of the Borders Railway to Hawick is a strong contender. There has long been discussion about reopening local stations on the West Coast Main Line (WCML) at Symington, Thankerton and Beattock, and a long-running campaign exists to reopen the line between Leuchars and the university town of St Andrews in Fife. Further electrification is probable on some Glasgow area suburban routes, notably to East Kilbride, Barrhead and Kilmarnock. A new station on the Glasgow-Neilston line to the south of Barrhead is under consideration. But a rail link of some sort to Glasgow Airport continues to be discussed, though it seems little further forward since its 2009 cancellation due to spending cuts. But otherwise the momentum for continuing rail improvements shows little sign of abating. There is pressure in some quarters to reintroduce passenger services to the 'City Union' line across Glasgow, which would enable through running between lines to the south-west and north-east of the city. But this would come at a cost of avoiding parts of the city centre, and overcoming capacity problems on the routes to be linked.

When I wrote the foregoing in August 2019 the future looked bright and the spectre of the wretched Covid-19 pandemic had not entered anyone's mind. Now, 12 months later, as trains run largely empty, the system is in effect re-nationalised, and the future is uncertain. The gloom and doom merchants say that public transport is finished, working from home will become the 'new normal', and consequently there is no need for any of the proposed developments mentioned above, as we'll all be confined to our homes for the foreseeable future. At the other end of the scale, the optimists say that once the pandemic is over – whenever, or if ever, that may be – things will quickly bounce back to 2019 levels. The Scottish Government clearly has faith in its rail network as it has recently announced, as a 'decarbonisation' measure, aspirations to electrify to just about everywhere, with the exception of the lightly used remote lines to Stranraer, Fort William, Oban and Mallaig, and to Kyle of Lochalsh and the Far North. My view is that usage levels will return, but goodness knows what the timescale will be.

I have given much consideration to a logical way in which to set out the order of stations and lines appearing in this book. Scottish local government is complex, and railways confuse matters further by crossing boundaries at inconvenient moments! Starting in the north, I've used the Scottish regions – Highland, Tayside, Stirling, etc – as a basis, but I've put the West Highland lines in a section by themselves, and have listed Greater Glasgow and Edinburgh/Lothians separately. Where lines cross boundaries I've placed them in the region with the most stations on that route. I hope this makes sense!

In previous volumes in the 'Passengers Once More' series the current operator of a new station has been shown. This has been omitted in this volume, as the operator of all the new stations, with the exception of heritage lines, is Abellio ScotRail. Heritage line stations are operated by the railways concerned. The original operator shown is the company prior to the 1923 Grouping.

The reference following each new station refers to the page reference and grid square in Stuart Baker's *Rail Atlas of Britain*, 14th edition. Some stations are not shown in Baker's atlas; in this case the approximate reference is shown in brackets. Where a 'P&P' entry is shown, this refers to photographs of the station listed in Silver Link's excellent 'British Railways Past and Present' series.

While a brief summary of passenger services

is shown for each station, intending visitors should check the current ScotRail timetable before travelling. Most, but not all, timetables have returned to something approaching normality after the initial Covid-19 outbreak in Spring 2020.

Most stations in Scotland have the station nameboards in Gaelic as well as English, although Gaelic is very rarely spoken outside the North West and the Western Isles. For those who are interested, a list of those stations with their Gaelic translations appears in the TRACKmaps 'Quail' book of railway track diagrams, book 1, which covers Scotland and the Isle of Man.

One of the problems I've encountered in photographing many modern stations is adding a degree of individuality to the pictures, given that most are constructed from standard components, architecture, disabled facilities, corporate signage, etc. As the current Abellio ScotRail blue corporate 'Saltire' scheme does nothing to highlight differences between train types, I make no apology for including trains in the pictures that are not representative of those that regularly use the station or line depicted; these might be steam specials, freights, excursions, or trains operated by another TOC. There are also some pictures that serve to illustrate stations with no train included, while some of the older photos illustrate various livery styles that have adorned Scottish trains over the last few years.

Scottish standard-gauge heritage lines that offer regular services have been included. The Strathspey Railway makes steady progress with its ultimate aim of reaching Grantown-on-Spey, where a new station slightly further south of the original will be constructed. The fledgling Royal Deeside line at Milton of Crathes will no doubt reach Banchory. Neither the Bo'ness & Kinneil Railway nor the Caledonian Railway at Brechin currently offer definite extension plans. And I've recently discovered an even more fledgling scheme at Invergarry in the Western Highlands. The preservation movement has proved numerous times that anything is possible, and hopefully the ravages of the wretched Covid-19 to their income will not prove to be fatal.

This is the last book in the 'Passengers Once More' series. Series editor Terry Gough had done much of the groundwork and research and had taken a great many of the photographs. I've collated Terry's material, added a little bit more here and there, photographed those locations Terry had not visited, mainly in the Glasgow area, and re-photographed some locations where the weather gods had not shined brightly on Terry's efforts or the scene has altered considerably since his initial visit. Terry was unable to complete this book and asked me to carry it forward, which I have great pleasure in so doing. I do hope you enjoy it and find it a useful point of reference.

Sadly Terry passed away in May 2019. It's my intention to donate any royalties received from the sale of this book to Prostate Cancer UK.

Bob Avery
Carluke, Lanarkshire
September 2020

Acknowledgements

The help and assistance of numerous people in helping me with this task is gratefully acknowledged. Primarily this was providing, confirming and clarifying information. Many people have helped with this, but in particular I'd like to thank my friends and former colleagues – in particular Jim Summers, Alan Mackie, Craig Crawford, Graham Maxtone, Bob Watt, Matt Monger, Dave Davidson, Craig Reilly, Keith Jones and Robin Ralston. Also a big thanks to Paul Strathdee, Jim Nisbet, Graham Maxtone, Mike Cooper and Steven Mackay, who have made photos available that fill in the gaps not filled by Terry or myself. I'd also like to acknowledge the help given by my father, Dr Donald Avery, in proof reading and some constructive suggestions, most of which have been incorporated.

HIGHLAND STATIONS

Alness		64 C1
Opened	23 May 1863	
Closed	13 June 1960	
Operator	Original – HR	
Reopened	7 May 1973	

Alness is located on Scotland's Far North Line to Wick and Thurso. It was reopened by BR as a result of housing development nearby. There are eight trains to Inverness daily, with five on Sundays. Heading north, there are eight trains daily, of which only four go the whole distance to Wick, with others terminating at Invergordon, Tain and Ardgay. On Sundays there are five trains southbound and six trains northbound, of which only one goes the whole distance.

Alness, looking towards Invergordon on 25 June 2012. *Terry Gough*

Alness, looking towards Inverness on the same day. It's 1230, with 2 hours and 11 minutes to wait before the next train (to Wick). *Terry Gough*

The station entrance, shelter and cycle storage facilities. *Terry Gough*

Beauly		60 C2
Opened	11 June 1862	
Closed	13 June 1960	
Reopened	15 April 2002	
Operator	original HR	

This tiny station, the first stop north of Inverness (west as the crow flies) is reported to have the shortest platform in the UK at 49.4 feet, long enough for one set of doors on a Class 158 DMU. It reopened after a successful local effort and reportedly resulted in a considerable swing from road to rail for local commuters to Inverness. Southbound it enjoys 13 tpd to Inverness and 11 in the opposite direction, with two of these going to Wick, four to Kyle of Lochalsh, one to Dingwall, one to Invergordon, one to Ardgay and two to Tain. On Sundays there are six trains to Inverness, while in the other direction there is one to Kyle of Lochalsh, one to Wick, one to Invergordon and three to Tain.

No 158713 leaves the tiny platform at Beauly for Inverness on 27 June 2012. *Terry Gough*

Highland stations

Above: Beauly, looking towards Dingwall on the same day. *Terry Gough*

Right: The station sign. 27 June 2012. *Terry Gough*

Below: A passenger waits for a northbound service. *Terry Gough*

Beauly
A'Mhanachainn

Conon Bridge		60 C2
Previous name	Conon	
Opened	11 June 1862	
Closed	13 June 1960	
Reopened	8 February 2013	
Operator	**original** HR	

Another resurrection of a Beeching era closure, this station also has a short platform, though fractionally longer than that at Beauly. This station was opened in time for major road disruption in the area caused by resurfacing on the Kessock Bridge. Train services are similar to those listed for Beauly.

Left: 'B1' Class 4-6-0 No 1306 *Mayflower* – en route with a railtour from Inverness to Kyle of Lochalsh – passes the short station platform of Conon Bridge on 11 May 2019. *Bob Avery*

Below: No 158703 draws into the tiny platform forming the 06.18 Wick-Inverness service on the same day. *Bob Avery*

Highland stations

Duncraig		63 C1
Previous name	Duncraig Platform	
Opened	2 November 1897	
Closed	7 December 1964	
Reopened	5 January 1976	
Operator	**original** HR	

This tiny isolated station on Loch Carron's southern shore was originally a private halt serving the nearby Duncraig Castle. The 12-year closure was official in nature but not in practice, and reopening came about, according to legend, as official recognition of traincrews repeatedly dropping people off there by request. Its tiny octagonal waiting room has Grade B listed status. There are four trains each way between Inverness and Kyle of Lochalsh, with just two on Sundays, reduced to one each way during the winter.

No 158719 leaves the tiny station at Duncraig forming a service from Kyle of Lochalsh to Inverness on 23 June 2012. *Terry Gough*

The picturesque and well-hidden station at Duncraig on the Inverness-Kyle of Lochalsh line, with its Grade B listed octagonal waiting room. *Terry Gough*

Dunrobin Castle		64 B1
Previous name	Dunrobin	
Opened	1 November 1870	
Closed	19 June 1871 (to become a private station)	
Closed completely	29 January 1965	
Reopened	30 June 1985	
Operator	**original** Duke of Sutherland's estate (HR)	

Dunrobin Castle, with its attractive Grade B listed building, was originally a private station for use by the Duke of Sutherland, his family, and visitors to the nearby castle. It's now a public station, near the village of Golspie. Despite its public status it only enjoys a service of three Wick-Inverness trains a day in each direction (just one each way on Sundays) between March and late October each year.

Above: The station sign, in its unique style. *Terry Gough*

Above right: 'B1' Class No 1306 *Mayflower* pauses at Dunrobin Castle, en route from Inverness to Brora with the 'Highlands and Islands' railtour on 11 May 2019. The isolated stretch of track in the foreground is a recreation of a siding where the Duke of Sutherland stabled his private saloon, which was, at his whim, attached to trains to Inverness and sometimes as far as London. *Bob Avery*

Right: A southbound Wick-Inverness service calls at Dunrobin Castle on 26 June 2012. *Terry Gough*

Highland stations

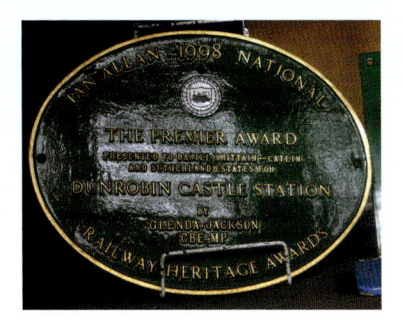

A plaque presented to Catlin and Sutherland Estates by Ian Allan Publishing/Railway Heritage Awards in 1998. *Terry Gough*

Dunrobin Castle's station building photographed on 11 May 2019. *Bob Avery*

Lochluichart		63 C2
Previous name	Lochluichart High	
Opened	1 August 1871 (originally as a private station)	
Closed	3 May 1954	
Reopened (on new site)	3 May 1954	
Operator	**original** HR	

The new station was necessitated by the realignment of the railway around the raised shores of Loch Luichart due to a hydro-electric scheme. Four trains between Inverness and Kyle of Lochalsh call each day, with one (two during the summer) on Sundays. All trains call by request.

'B1' No 61306 *Mayflower* approaches Lochluichart en route from Inverness to Kyle of Lochalsh on 12 May 2019. *Bob Avery*

An unpaved road leads to the lochside and the station entrance at Lochluichart. *Bob Avery*

Muir of Ord		63 C2
Opened	11 June 1862	
Closed	13 June 1960	
Reopened	4 October 1976	
Operator	original HR	

Train services are as shown for Beauly. The station achieved some notoriety when it became the temporary maintenance depot for trains from Kyle of Lochalsh and the Far North line after Inverness's Ness River rail bridge was swept away in February 1989, isolating these lines from the rest of the network. The new replacement bridge opened in 1990.

Left and below left: No 158718 calls at Muir of Ord as the 08.55 Inverness-Kyle of Lochalsh service on 11 May 2019. Most of the passengers are waiting for a following steam special to Kyle of Lochalsh. *Bob Avery*

The station sign, 27 June 2012. *Terry Gough*

Below: A glimpse through the up-side entrance shows No 158715 calling as the 08.55 Inverness-Kyle service on 11 May 2019. *Bob Avery*

Highland stations

Rogart		64 B1
Previous names	Rogart, Rogart Halt	
Opened	13 July 1868	
Closed	13 June 1960	
Reopened	12 June 1961	
Operator	**original** HR	

The station was reopened as a result of local pressure after just a year of closure. Four trains daily call each way between Wick and Inverness, reducing to one each way on Sundays. Budget accommodation is available at the station in two former BR Mark 2 carriages.

Above: An 'A1' on the Far North line? No 60163 *Tornado* pauses briefly at Rogart en route from Inverness to Brora on 21 June 2015. *Bob Avery*

Right: A Class 158 unit pauses at Rogart on its long journey south on 26 June 2012. *Terry Gough*

Invergarry (Invergarry & Fort Augustus Railway Museum)		60 A1
Opened	22 July 1903	
Closed	1 December 1933	
Reopened	2019	
Operator	**original** NBR	

Scotland's newest preserved station is on the former branch line between Spean Bridge and Fort Augustus, in the Great Glen – a one-time part of the NBR's plan to reach Inverness to rival the Highland Railway. It is primarily a railway museum, but warrants inclusion here as it boasts a few hundred yards of track and offers rides in a motorised permanent way trolley or a Ruston diesel locomotive on selected days each year. The (not publicly stated) prospect of further extensions is mouth-watering.

General views of the fledgling Invergarry & Fort Augustus Railway Museum, where rides are offered on selected operating days each year.
Both Graham Maxtone

STRATHSPEY RAILWAY

Aviemore Speyside (Strathspey Railway)	
Opened	22 July 1978
Closed	July 1998
Operator	**original** Strathspey Railway

This was the preserved Strathspey Railway's first station in Aviemore. It was built with components from Dalnaspidal, a former station on the Perth-Inverness Highland main line, which had succumbed to Beeching in May 1965. Strathspey Railway trains transferred to the main station in Aviemore in 1998, giving easier access from the town and better connections from main-line trains. Speyside station's infrastructure was initially retained in case problems should develop with the Network Rail connection in future years, eventually succumbing to demolition in 2013.

'B1' No 1306 *Mayflower* heads the 'Highlands and Islands' railtour away from Aviemore to the south on the Highland main line on 13 May 2019. The Strathspey's current platform is on the right, through the crossing gates. The original (now disused) Strathspey heritage line station is in the far distance, just out of sight. *Bob Avery*

The Strathspey Railway's Aviemore (Speyside) station served as the heritage line's southern terminus for 20 years from 1978 until services were diverted into the railway's own platform at Aviemore station (shared with ScotRail). Components of the station building originated at Dalnaspidal, further south on the Highland main line. *Terry Gough*

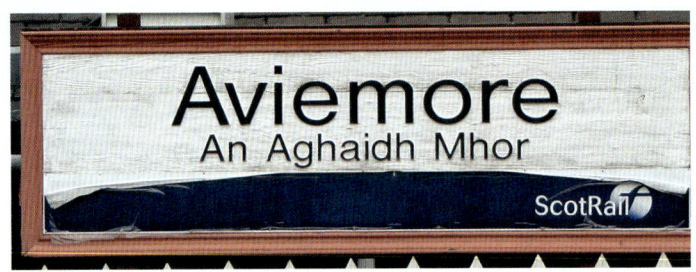

Left: The Aviemore station sign, photographed on 28 June 2012 and showing Abellio's predecessor as holder of the ScotRail franchise. *Terry Gough*

Below: The National Railway Museum's No 3440 *City of Truro*, on holiday in Scotland, leaves Aviemore with the 14.45 service to Broomhill on 6 September 2006, with the Cairngorm range in the background. *Bob Avery*

Strathspey Railway

Boat of Garten (Strathspey Railway)		
Opened	3 August 1863	
Closed	18 October 1965	
Reopened	22 July 1978	
Operator	**original** HR/GNSR	

This is the main station, locomotive depot and headquarters of what is now the Strathspey Railway tourist line. The original station building survives and enjoys Category B listed status.

Left: A Strathspey Railway train is about to leave Boat of Garten for Broomhill, circa 2004. *Bob Avery*

Below: The attractive station buildings at Boat of Garten, looking south towards Aviemore on 28 June 2012. *Terry Gough*

Broomhill (Strathspey Railway)	
Previous name	Broomhill for Nethy Bridge
Opened	3 August 1863
Closed	18 October 1965
Reopened	31 May 2002
Operator	*original* HR

This is currently the northern terminus of the Strathspey Railway tourist line, which is in the process of extending further north to Grantown-on-Spey.

The Strathspey Railway's Caledonian Railway 0-6-0 No 828 stands at the line's current northern terminus at Broomhill on 28 June 2012. *Terry Gough*

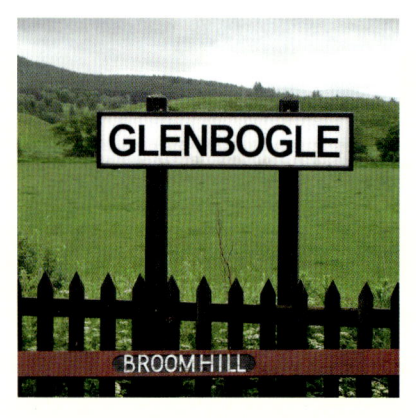

The Strathspey Railway's Broomhill station featured as 'Glenbogle' in the BBC TV series *Monarch of the Glen*. A station nameboard is retained to mark its role in the programme. *Terry Gough*

No 828 runs tender-first into Broomhill with a train from Aviemore on 28 June 2012. *Terry Gough*

MORAYSHIRE STATIONS
(Keith & Dufftown Railway)

Dufftown (Keith & Dufftown Railway)		64 C2
Opened	21 February 1862	
Closed	6 May 1968	
Reopened	2000	
Operator	*original* GNSR	

This is the headquarters of the Keith & Dufftown Railway, which runs diesel services between March and September, weekends only (including Fridays in the summer months).

The Keith & Dufftown Railway's Dufftown station building on 29 June 2012. *Terry Gough*

The Keith & Dufftown Railway's resident Class 108 DMU waits between trips at the railway's Dufftown station on the same day. *Terry Gough*

Drummuir (Keith & Dufftown Railway)		64 C2
Opened	21 February 1862	
Closed	6 May 1968	
Reopened	2000	
Operator	*original* GNSR	

The location of the main intermediate station on this heritage line is peaceful and idyllic, and is a good kicking-off point for many walks in the area.

Left and opposite top: The Keith & Dufftown Railway's Class 108 DMU calls at the leafy, idyllic Drummuir station on 29 June 2012. *Both Terry Gough*

Morayshire stations (Keith & Dufftown Railway)

Towiemore (Keith & Dufftown Railway)		64 C2
Opened	May 1926	
Closed	6 May 1968	
Reopened	2000	
Operator	*original* LNER	

This tiny station is listed as a request stop on the Keith & Dufftown line. It lacks necessities such as a platform, and not surprisingly sees little use.

The Keith & Dufftown Railway's regular Class 108 DMU stands at Keith Town station in between runs to Dufftown (away from camera) on 29 June 2012 *Terry Gough*

Keith Town (Keith and Dufftown Railway)		64 C2
Previous name	Earlsmill	
Opened	18 August 1858	
Closed	6 May 1968	
Reopened	2005	
Operator	original GNSR	

The northern terminus of the Keith & Dufftown Railway is convenient for Keith town centre. The railway has aspirations of reconnecting to the national network at Keith station, some half a mile to the north.

Looking on the opposite direction, the line carries on in the distance and forms a rarely used connection to Network Rail metals. *Terry Gough*

ABERDEENSHIRE STATIONS

Dyce		62 A2
Opened	17 July 1861	
Closed	6 May 1968	
Reopened	15 September 1984	
Operator	original GNSR	

The GNSR's former line to Peterhead and Fraserburgh branched off here. It now serves a northern Aberdeen suburb and Aberdeen Airport, to which it is linked by a bus shuttle. There's an hourly service each way, to Aberdeen and points south in one direction and to Inverurie (and some trains continuing to Inverness) in the other. At the time of writing it seems that service frequency will be further improved in the near future.

Right: This view of Dyce station on 15 August 2019, in the throes of a two-week shutdown for track and signalling improvements, shows its proximity to Aberdeen Airport. The aircraft is a Fokker 100 belonging to TradeAir, a Croatian charter operator. *Bob Avery*

Below: Looking towards Aberdeen on the same day, an impressive signal box once dominated this view, but it was demolished earlier. *Bob Avery*

Kintore		62 A1
Opened	20 September 1854	
Closed	7 December 1964	
Reopened	15 October 2020	
Operator	original GNSR	

Reopening had been scheduled for May 2020, but was postponed due to Covid-19. Train services are similar to those shown for Dyce.

Left: The new station at Kintore is under construction in this view looking south-east towards Aberdeen on 15 August 2019. *Bob Avery*

Below: A rarity at Kintore – an LNER 'Azuma', which has found itself on the wrong side of the tragic Stonehaven blockage, makes its way south via Inverness on 20 August 2020. The station opened the following October. *Mike Cooper*

Aberdeenshire stations

Portlethen		62 B2
Opened	1 April 1850	
Closed	11 June 1956	
Reopened	17 May 1985	
Operator	original CR	

The new station (slightly further south than the original) serves a burgeoning village south of Aberdeen. It now enjoys an improved frequency of an hourly service each way between Aberdeen (connections to Inverurie and Inverness) and Montrose (where connections further south are available). There are six northbound and five southbound trains on Sundays, with the southbound trains going forward to Edinburgh and one to Perth.

A plaque acknowledging finance for the station reopening. *Terry Gough*

Portlethen Station opened by Councillor Ian B Robertson Chairman, Transportation and Roads Committee Grampian Regional Council in recognition of the financial contribution made by Grampian Regional Council to the construction of this station 17-5-85 ScotRail

A Class 158 and 170 combination – common on Inverness and Aberdeen services – passes southbound through Portlethen on 1 July 2012. *Terry Gough*

Laurencekirk		62 C1
Opened	1 November 1849	
Closed	4 September 1967	
Reopened	18 May 2009	
Operator	**original** CR	

A success story brought about by local pressure, this station now enjoys at least twice its original estimated patronage. A basic hourly service in each direction runs between Aberdeen and Montrose (where connections are available for major cities further south). A new 'Aberdeen Crossrail' service under development may see northbound trains extended beyond Aberdeen to Inverurie. On Sundays the service is less frequent but southbound services run through to Glasgow or Edinburgh.

Below: An Aberdeen-bound 'Turbostar' calls at Laurencekirk on 1 May 2019. *Bob Avery*

Aberdeenshire stations

31

Above: John Cameron's 'A4' 'Pacific' No 60009 *Union of South Africa* romps through Laurencekirk bound for Aberdeen with the 'Great Britain XII' railtour on 1 May 2019. *Bob Avery*

Below: The Laurencekirk down-side station building, photographed on 1 July 2012. *Terry Gough*

ROYAL DEESIDE RAILWAY

Milton of Crathes		62 B1
Previous name	Crathes Castle, Crathes	
Opened	8 September 1853	
Closed	28 February 1966	
Reopened	2010	
Operator	*original* GNSR	

The Royal Deeside Railway is one of Britain's newer heritage lines, having commenced operations in 2010. The current station is a new one; the original is approximately a quarter of a mile further east and is not considered practical for today's operations. This is the main station on the line, though there are aspirations to reach Banchory, some 2 miles to the west. A new platform, to be called 'West Lodge', marks the current limit of operations towards Banchory, though there are currently no access facilities.

Drewry Class 03 diesel shunter No D2094 with three Mark 2 coaches stands at Milton of Crathes station on the Royal Deeside Railway, near Banchory, Aberdeenshire, on 15 August 2019. *Bob Avery*

ANGUS STATIONS
(Caledonian Railway (Brechin) Ltd)

Brechin (Caledonian Railway (Brechin) Ltd)		62 C1
Opened	1 February 1848	
Closed	4 August 1952	
Reopened	1981	
Operator	**original** CR	

This is the headquarters and main station of this heritage line. Trains ran within the station area once BR had closed the line to freight in 1981, then operations over the full 4 miles to Bridge of Dun commenced in 1993.

A general view of the Caledonian Railway's station and yard at Brechin, seen on the same day. *Terry Gough*

The station platform.
Terry Gough

Below: An external view of Brechin station on 1 July 2012. *Terry Gough*

Angus stations (Caledonian Railway (Brechin) Ltd)

Bridge of Dun (Caledonian Railway (Brechin) Ltd)		62 C1
Opened	1 February 1848	
Closed	4 September 1967	
Reopened	1993	
Operator	original CR	

This is the other end of what is now the Brechin to Bridge of Dun heritage line.

Above: The Caledonian Railway (Brechin) station at Bridge of Dun on 1 July 2012. *Terry Gough*

TAYSIDE STATIONS

Balmossie		61 B2
Previous name	Balmossie Halt	
Opened	18 June 1962	
Operator	original BR	

This station originally served local trains between Dundee and Arbroath, which ended in 1990. Since then it has had only two trains in each direction (nothing on Sundays). The reasons for its ludicrously sparse service are not clear, as it lies in a residential area north of Dundee.

This is Balmossie, near Carnoustie on the north bank of the Tay, looking south-west towards Dundee on 1 July 2012. *Terry Gough*

Looking north-east towards Arbroath on the same day.
Terry Gough

CrossCountry's 08.20 Aberdeen-Penzance service, formed of the usual 'Voyager' diesel unit, speeds south through Balmossie on 15 August 2019. *Bob Avery*

The tiny halt at Balmossie is seen again, looking north, on the same day. The platform indicator indicates the sparse nature of the train service. *Bob Avery*

Golf Street		61 B2
Previous name	Golf Street Halt	
Opened	7 November 1960	
Operator	original BR	

Golf Street has a sad story similar to that of Balmossie, with a similar train service, though it does have the distinction of having been used by additional services for the Open Golf Championship at Carnoustie in 1999.

Golf Street, looking towards Aberdeen on 1 July 2012. *Terry Gough*

Golf Street station entrance on the down (northbound) side. *Terry Gough*

The 09.04 Aberdeen-Edinburgh service, formed of one of ScotRail's refurbished 'InterCity' HSTs, speeds south through Golf Street on 15 August 2019. *Bob Avery*

FIFE STATIONS

Dalgety Bay		57 A1
Previous name	Donibristle Halt	
Opened	1942	
Closed	2 November 1959	
Reopened	27 March 1998	
Operator	original LNER	

The short-lived Donibristle Halt was named after the Earl of Moray's Donibristle estate, on whose land it stood. Little trace remains today; it is thought that the current 1998 station occupies a site very close by. It now serves residential and light industrial development and a small beach area. A basic half-hourly service operates between Edinburgh and Glenrothes with Thornton, with alternate northbound trains continuing beyond Glenrothes to return to Edinburgh via Dunfermline. In the evening trains run to Dundee or Perth. On Sundays the service is hourly to Glenrothes, with early and late through services to Dundee.

No 158712 accelerates away from Dalgety Bay with a Fife Circle service bound for Edinburgh on 6 July 2012. *Terry Gough*

Car parking, cycle storage and easy drop-off facilities at Dalgety Bay. *Terry Gough*

Fife stations

Dunfermline Queen Margaret		57 A1
Opened	26 January 2000	
Operator	**original** ScotRail (National Express)	

This modern station serves the eastern end of Dunfermline, the nearby hospital (after which it is named) and a superstore, and is approximately a mile from the M9 motorway. There's a basic half-hourly service in each direction, with alternate eastbound trains proceeding beyond Cowdenbeath to Glenrothes with Thornton (see separate listing) back to Edinburgh via Kirkcaldy. In the evening service frequency decreases to hourly, and on Sundays there is an hourly service between Glenrothes and Edinburgh only.

Above: Class 158 and 170 units, both decked in First Group's 'Barbie' livery, pass at Dunfermline Queen Margaret on 6 July 2012. *Terry Gough*

Right: An anti-clockwise Fife Circle service runs into Dunfermline Queen Margaret, bound for Edinburgh via Rosyth, on 6 June 2012. *Terry Gough*

Glenrothes with Thornton		57 A1
Opened	11 May 1992	
Operator	**original** BR	

This station is situated at the north end of the 'Fife Circle', just west of its triangular junction with the Edinburgh-Aberdeen main line between Kirkcaldy and Markinch. It serves Glenrothes new town and the former mining community of Thornton. Its layout is unusual, as the apparent double track is in fact two parallel single lines. The station boasts three tph to Edinburgh, two of which run via Kirkcaldy and the other via Dunfermline. In the evenings trains run via Dunfermline only. Sundays see two tph to Edinburgh, alternating between Kirkcaldy and Dunfermline routings. In addition there is a very limited service to Perth. All trains except those to/from Perth use Platform 1.

Right: Complications arise from having two parallel single lines running through Glenrothes with Thornton station! *Terry Gough*

Below: A service for Edinburgh via Dunfermline has just left Platform 1 on 6 July 2012. *Terry Gough*

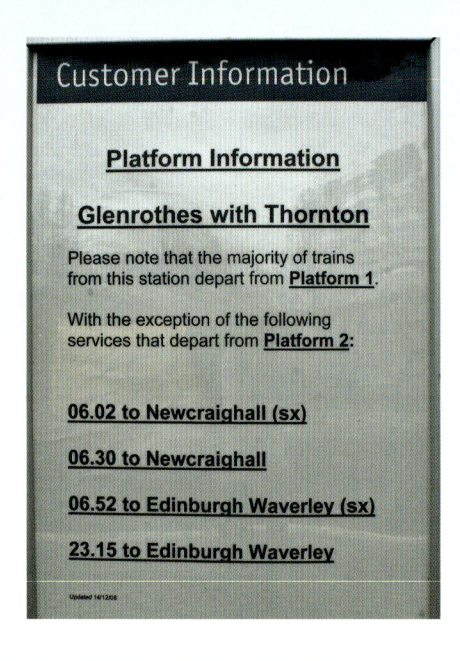

Customer Information

Platform Information

Glenrothes with Thornton

Please note that the majority of trains from this station depart from **Platform 1**.

With the exception of the following services that depart from **Platform 2:**

06.02 to Newcraighall (sx)

06.30 to Newcraighall

06.52 to Edinburgh Waverley (sx)

23.15 to Edinburgh Waverley

Fife stations

Culross (temporary station)		56 A2
Opened	1 July 1906	
Closed	7 July 1930	
Reopened	21 June 1992	
Closed	2 August 1992	
Operator	**original** NBR	

The original line from Alloa to Dunfermline along the north bank of the Firth of Forth lost its passenger service long ago, and from 1970 until 2016 was used for heavy coal traffic to Longannet and Kincardine power stations. Culross is a picturesque village favoured by day-trippers, and the temporary 1992 platform adjacent to the car park was used by special trains to an event within Longannet power station. No trace of the original station remains. The coal traffic has now ceased and the line sees little use, but there is some prospect of a reinstated passenger service in years to come.

Above: LNER Class 'K4' 2-6-0 No 61994 *The Great Marquess* runs through Culross to much acclaim from onlookers with a Scottish Railway Preservation Society Forth Circle railtour on 22 August 2010. *Bob Avery*

Below: Seen from the location of Culross temporary station, No 56048 wheels coal empties away from Longannet power station along the north bank of the Firth of Forth towards Dunfermline on 8 November 1996. Coal trains and Longannet power station itself are now history, but passenger trains may grace this line some time in the future. *Bob Avery*

Right: Unit No 150259 stands at the temporary platform at Culross, forming a shuttle service into Longannet power station on the occasion of the open day there on 21 June 1992. *Jim Nisbet*

Below: Crowds gather for the Longannet open day in the car park at Culross. The picture was taken from the temporary platform, complete with official station sign. *Jim Nisbet*

Perth to Ladybank Line   61 C1

The Perth (Hilton Junction) to Ladybank link lost its passenger services in 1955, but regained them on 6 October 1975 when some Edinburgh to Perth and Inverness services were routed this way. There are no intermediate stations and the line is single track throughout. Now an hourly Edinburgh-Perth service each way uses this line, as well as the occasional railtour and freight service.

Class 40 No 40145 heads defective 'Deltic' No 55022 and a return Railway Touring Company Inverness-King's Cross special at Easter Cluny, on the Perth-Ladybank single line, on 9 October 2006. *Bob Avery*

STIRLING AREA STATIONS

Alloa		60 C2
Opened	28 August 1850	
Closed	7 October 1968	
Reopened	15 May 2008	
P&P	No 9 p84	
Operator	**original** NBR	

15 May 2008 was the official reopening date, but train services started four days later on Monday 19. The new station is on a site approximately a quarter of a mile east of its original location. Centrally funded by the Scottish Government, a major factor in the decision to reopen was to allow a more direct route for coal trains bound for Longannet power station (which have now ceased following Longannet's closure in March 2016), which would free up a number of paths over the Forth Bridge.

There is an hourly service to Glasgow Queen Street seven days a week, which attracts considerable patronage, higher than initial forecasts. Additionally a peak-hour weekday service to Edinburgh and return is offered. Following wiring, electric services commenced in December 2018.

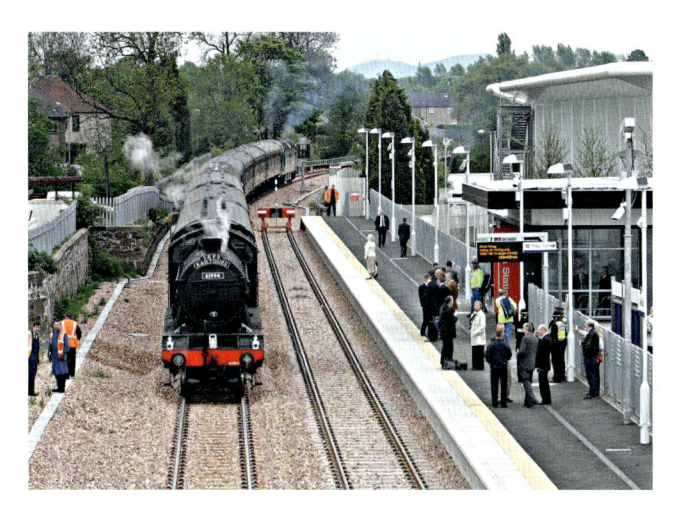

Left: No 61994 *The Great Marquess*, with 'Deltic' No 55022 at the rear, stands alongside the new Alloa station with empty stock for the reopening special on 15 May 2008. The line the train is standing on continues to Longannet power station (now defunct), Culross and Dunfermline. *Bob Avery*

Below: 'Turbostar' No 170459 stands in the single-platform terminus line at Alloa on 3 July 2012, prior to working to Stirling and Glasgow Queen Street. The through track is the freight line to Longannet power station and Dunfermline. There are aspirations for a reintroduction of a passenger service east of Alloa. *Terry Gough*

Bridge of Allan		60 C2
Opened	22 May 1848	
Closed	1 November 1965	
Reopened	13 May 1985	
P&P	No 9 p89	
Operator	original CR	

The original station lies to the north of the A9 road, the new station to the south. The station serves a very pleasant town with commuting potential to Glasgow, Edinburgh and nearby Stirling, and is convenient for Stirling University campus. Three tph operate in each direction – southbound trains to Edinburgh (two tph) and Glasgow (one tph). Northbound trains go to Dunblane, with occasional services to Perth, Dundee and Inverness. The line was electrified in 2018 and most trains are now formed of new Class 385 EMUs.

Right: A pre-electrification view of Bridge of Allan, with 158 871 leaving for Dunblane on 3 July 2012. *Terry Gough*

Below: 'Just out of the box', unit No 385123 forms an Edinburgh to Dunblane working on 14 March 2019. *Bob Avery*

Stirling area stations

No 170404 hurries through Bridge of Allan with a Glasgow to Aberdeen working on the same day. *Bob Avery*

Car parking at Bridge of Allan in 2019, already showing evidence of being insufficient. *Bob Avery*

Camelon		56 A2
Previous names	Camelon, Falkirk (Camelon)	
Opened	October 1844	
Closed	4 September 1967	
Reopened	4 October 1994	
Operator	**original** NBR	

The new station is approximately 250 yards west of the original, which had an island platform, and the present separate alignment of the up and down lines, which widen at the east end of the present station, marks the site of the original. Camelon enjoys two tph from Edinburgh to Dunblane, and a further two tph to Glasgow Queen Street via Cumbernauld. In the reverse direction this equates to four tph to Falkirk Grahamston, Linlithgow and Edinburgh. On Sundays there are two tph to Edinburgh, with alternate westbound trains to Dunblane and Stirling, with no service to Glasgow. The station lies within sight of Carmuirs East Junction, where lines to Stirling and Glasgow split. Freight trains to and from Grangemouth docks and refinery pass through the station. The line is now electrified.

This is Camelon, looking east, on 3 July 2012. Many Scottish stations feature these rather cumbersome footbridges to benefit people with luggage, prams etc, or who are disabled. But not all have received this rather attractive green colour scheme. Electrification has now altered this scene considerably. *Terry Gough*

48   Passengers Once More

Looking west, 'Turbostar' No 170421 arrives at Camelon with a Glasgow Queen Street to Falkirk Grahamston working on the same day. Terry Gough

ARGYLL/LOCHABER (WEST HIGHLAND LINES)

Loch Awe		60 C1
Opened	1 July 1880	
Closed	1 November 1965	
Reopened	10 May 1985	
P&P	No 31 p52	
Operator	original CR	

This reopening serves the nearby village, popular with tourists. Six tph each way link Glasgow with Oban, reduced to three on Sundays, with four during the summer.

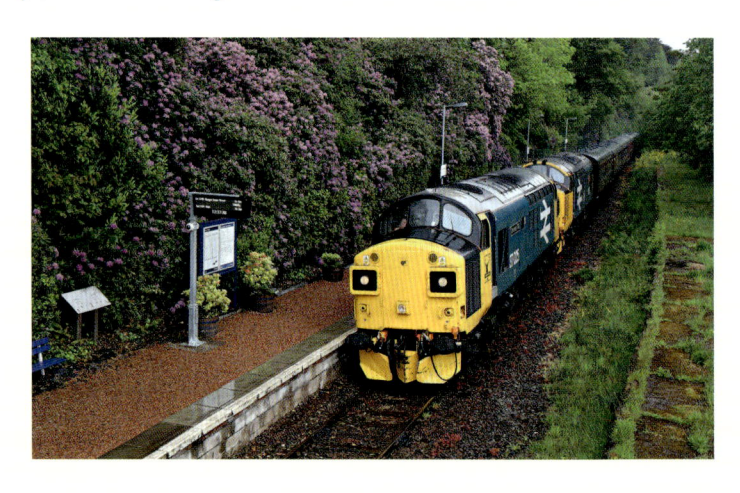

Nos 37025/402 head a Newcastle-Oban railtour through Loch Awe on 27 May 2019. Bob Avery

Argyll/Lochaber (West Highland lines)

The idyllic setting of Loch Awe station is famous for its rhododendron display. The remains of the former second platform are clearly visible on 12 June 2012. *Terry Gough*

A plaque commemorating the reopening. *Terry Gough*

Falls of Cruachan		60 B1
Opened	1 October 1893	
Closed	1 November 1965	
Reopened	20 June 1988	
Operator	**original** CR	

This reopening was a result of local initiative by BR's Area Business Group. The station is used mainly by hikers and visitors to the nearby hydro-electric power station. Trains call only during the summer months, as there is no station lighting. There are four trains to Glasgow and five to Oban each day, reducing to three each way on Sundays (one going to Crianlarich only, with a connection to Glasgow).

Falls of Cruachan station, looking west towards Oban on 12 June 2012. *Terry Gough*

A plaque marking the reopening of the station in 1988. *Terry Gough*

Loch Eil Outward Bound		60 B1
Opened	20 April 1985	
Operator	**original** BR	

The station was built to serve the nearby Outward Bound Centre, and sits in an idyllic location on the shores of Loch Eil. Four trains each way daily (three on Sundays) between Fort William and Mallaig call here. The famous 'Jacobite' steam service (summer only) passes but does not call.

A glimpse of the small station from the passing 'Jacobite' steam-hauled service on 21 June 2012 – locomotive not known! *Terry Gough*

Participants of activities at the Loch Eil Outward Bound centre gather near the small station that serves it. *Terry Gough*

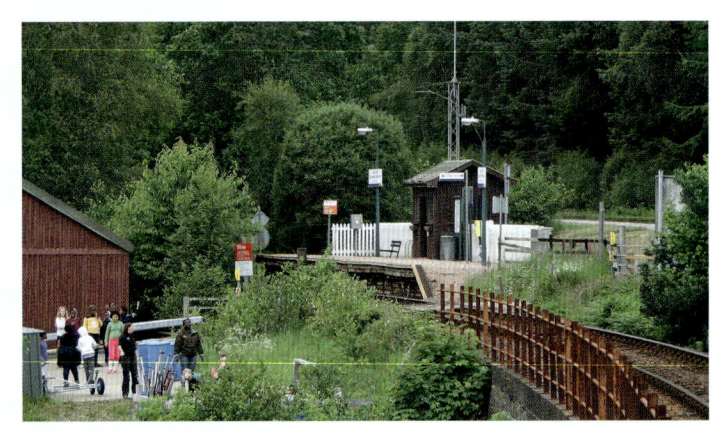

Looking east from the station towards Fort William, Ben Nevis dominates the skyline on 20 June 2012. *Terry Gough*

EDINBURGH AND LOTHIANS

Edinburgh to Airdrie via Bathgate

This corridor has seen considerable development since Edinburgh-Bathgate services were introduced by BR in 1986. The 'missing link' west of Bathgate opened in March 2011, providing an additional route between Glasgow and Edinburgh, and was electrified from the outset. Stations starting from the east end are listed in order. Stations at Drumgelloch and Airdrie are in fact in Greater Glasgow but form part of the Airdrie-Bathgate link, hence their inclusion here. All services are provided by Class 334 EMUs.

Edinburgh Park		57 A1
Opened	4 December 2003	
Operator	**original** ScotRail (National Express)	

This new station serves a business park of the same name, some nearby hotels and the Hermiston Gait retail park. It is adjacent to the Edinburgh Park stop on the Edinburgh Trams route from Edinburgh Airport to York Place, opened on 31 May 2014. Interchange between heavy and light rail is an easy process. The line through Edinburgh Park was electrified in October 2010 as part of the Airdrie-Bathgate link. Extensions to electrification in Central Scotland mean that most services serving Edinburgh Park are now electrically worked.

There are eight tph to Edinburgh Waverley. In a westerly direction, there are two tph to Helensburgh Central and two tph to Milngavie (both via Glasgow Queen Street Low Level), two tph to Dunblane via Stirling, and two tph to Glasgow Queen Street via Falkirk Grahamston.

Above: An Edinburgh-bound Class 334 unit arrives at Edinburgh Park station from the Bathgate line on 6 July 2012. At that time only Bathgate line services were electrically operated – following further electrification in central Scotland, the majority of trains serving this station are EMUs. Edinburgh's tram route to the airport is off picture to the left. *Terry Gough*

Left: Unit No 158723 pauses at Edinburgh Park, probably on a Dunblane working, on the same day. These services are now worked largely by brand-new Hitachi Class 385 EMUs. *Terry Gough*

Passengers Once More

Uphall		56 A2
Previous name	Houston	
Opened	1 August 1865	
Closed	9 January 1956	
Reopened	24 March 1986	
Operator	original NBR	

There is no trace of the original station. The current one was reopened as a single platform with the reintroduction of services between Edinburgh and Bathgate, and the second platform was brought into use in 2008. Electrification as part of the Airdrie-Bathgate project took place in 2010. The station is adjacent to the M8 motorway, and has car parking facilities. There are four tph to Edinburgh Waverley, two tph to Helensburgh Central and two tph to Milngavie. On Sundays a half-hourly service between Helensburgh Central and Edinburgh Waverley serves the station.

An Edinburgh-bound Class 334 unit heads east at Uphall on 6 July 2012. *Terry Gough*

A six-car Class 334 formation on an Edinburgh-Helensburgh working pauses at Uphall on the same day. Apart from the very occasional diversion or railtour, Class 334s have monopolised the Airdrie-Bathgate line since its opening. *Terry Gough*

Edinburgh and Lothians 53

Livingston North		56 A2
Opened	24 March 1986	
Operator	**original** BR	

The second platform was added in 2008. Services are as shown for Uphall.

Above: No 334006 accelerates away westwards from its station stop at Livingston North on 6 July 2012. *Terry Gough*

Left: On the same day No 334020 runs into the eastbound platform at Livingston North, amongst the clutter that typifies the modern Scottish station. *Terry Gough*

Passengers Once More

Bathgate		56 A2
Opened	24 March 1985	
Closed	16 October 2010	
Reopened (on new site)	18 October 2010	
P&P	No 9 pp100, 101	
Operator	*original* BR	

The new station (on a separate site from the NBR's original Bathgate Upper and Lower stations), opened as part of the Airdrie-Bathgate project, replacing the BR single-platform station of 1985 approximately a third of a mile to the north-west that was built as part of BR's original Edinburgh-Bathgate reopening scheme. The new station enjoys a similar service pattern to Uphall and Livingston North. A few early-morning and late-evening trains terminate at Bathgate because of its proximity to ScotRail's new EMU depot adjacent to the station. It has an extensive parking area but even this sometimes fills up on weekdays.

Above: The 1985 station at Bathgate is seen circa 2010; it closed in October of that year. No 158728 has arrived from Edinburgh and is boarding for the return trip. *Terry Gough*

Below: Bathgate depot (foreground) and new station under construction circa 2010. *Terry Gough*

Left: A westbound unit is about to leave Bathgate's Platform 2 with an Edinburgh-Helensburgh service on 6 July 2012. The EMU depot, which services Class 334s exclusively, is adjacent to the station on the left. *Terry Gough*

Below: No 334036 is about to depart towards Edinburgh. Bathgate's EMU depot is on the right. *Terry Gough*

Armadale		56 B2
Opened	11 August 1862	
Closed	9 January 1956	
Reopened	4 March 2011	
P&P	No 9 p103	
Operator	**original** NBR	

Armadale has a half-hourly service to Milngavie (via Glasgow Queen Street Low Level) to the west, and to Bathgate and Edinburgh to the east. On Sundays trains run to Helensburgh Central rather than Milngavie.

The modern sea of lamp posts, pre-cast bridges and shelters that makes up the modern ScotRail station at Armadale, seen on 6 July 2012, the date of all these views. *Terry Gough*

Above: Two Class 334 units in the erstwhile Strathclyde PTE crimson and cream scheme depart from Armadale towards Edinburgh. *Terry Gough*

Right: Unit 334017 is working a Helensburgh-Edinburgh service. *Terry Gough*

The station sign. *Terry Gough*

Armadale
Armadal

Blackridge		56 B2
Previous name	Westcraigs	
Opened	11 August 1862	
Closed	9 January 1956	
Reopened	12 December 2010	
Operator	**original** NBR	

The new station is some one-third of a mile further east than the original Westcraigs station. Train services are the same as for Armadale.

Looking east, Class 334s, displaying older and newer ScotRail liveries, pass at Blackridge on 6 July 2012. *Terry Gough*

Blackridge
An Druim Dubh

Above: The station sign. *Terry Gough*

Left: A platform view on the same day. *Terry Gough*

Caldercruix		56 B1
Opened	11 August 1862	
Closed	9 January 1956	
Reopened	13 February 2011	
Operator	**original** NBR	

Another new station on the Airdrie-Bathgate link. The train services are as listed for Armadale.

Eastbound and westbound Class 334s pass at Caldercruix on 6 July 2012. The pleasant carmine and cream livery is now extinct. *Terry Gough*

A peak-hour Edinburgh to Helensburgh service rolls into Caldercruix on the same day. *Terry Gough*

Drumgelloch		56 B1
Previous name	Clarkston, Clarkston (Lanarks)	
Opened	11 August 1862	
Closed	9 January 1956	
Reopened	15 May 1989	
Closed	9 May 2010	
Reopened	6 March 2011	
Operator	original NBR	

The station was reopened initially in 1989 as a short extension eastwards for North Clyde services formerly terminating at Airdrie. This single-platform structure was replaced by the current station 500 yards further east (on the site of the original Clarkston station) as part of the Airdrie-Bathgate project. Drumgelloch has a large car parking area and enjoys an excellent frequent train service, similar to that shown for Uphall. (Not to be confused with Clarkston station between Glasgow Central and East Kilbride.)

The station sign. *Terry Gough*

Liveried in Strathclyde Orange, Class 320 units approach Drumgelloch in September 1993 before the line was doubled and extended through to Bathgate. *Paul Strathdee*

The enlarged and double-tracked station at Drumgelloch is seen as a six-car Class 334 formation accelerates away for Airdrie, Glasgow Queen Street Low Level and Helensburgh on 6 July 2012. *Terry Gough*

The Borders Railway

Arguably Scotland's biggest rail renaissance in recent years is the Borders Railway, which links Edinburgh with Tweedbank in the Scottish Borders. It involved the reopening of the northern part of the former 'Waverley Route', which linked Carlisle with Edinburgh, but which was closed with much controversy in 1969. The reopening of the line reconnects the highly agreeable Borders area with the National Rail network. Services began in 2015, though stations at the Edinburgh area had reopened previously. Stations are listed from Edinburgh southwards. Provision was made at the outset for charter train operation and a number have been run since opening, bringing a number of preserved steam locomotives to the line.

Brunstane		68 C2
Opened	3 June 2002	
Operator	**original** ScotRail (National Express)	

In 2002 many trains from west of Edinburgh were extended to the east of the city to terminate at Newcraighall, calling at Brunstane's single platform en route. The station is located just off the ECML between Portobello and Niddrie South Junctions, and serves a residential area and nearby retail complex. Before 2015 it had a half-hourly service in each direction; since then the frequency has remained the same but has been incorporated into the Borders Railway timetable, with the addition of some peak-hour trains to/from Fife.

The 12.29 Tweedbank-Edinburgh service, formed of unit No 158741, calls at Brunstane, the penultimate stop on its journey, on 14 August 2019. *Bob Avery*

Newcraighall		68 C2
Previous name	Niddrie	
Opened	1 September 1848	
Closed	1 October 1860	
Reopened	1 December 1864	
Closed	1 February 1869	
Reopened	3 June 2002	
Operator	original NBR	

The precise site of the original Niddrie station, with its two short lives, is slightly to the north-west of the current station. The train service is as listed for Brunstane.

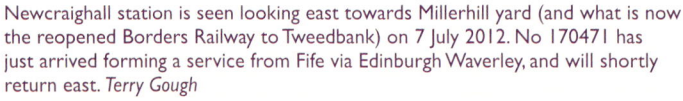

Newcraighall station is seen looking east towards Millerhill yard (and what is now the reopened Borders Railway to Tweedbank) on 7 July 2012. No 170471 has just arrived forming a service from Fife via Edinburgh Waverley, and will shortly return east. *Terry Gough*

With passenger numbers swelled considerably by the Edinburgh Festival, the 09.58 Tweedbank-Edinburgh service calls at Newcraighall on 8 August 2019. *Bob Avery*

Newcraighall
Talla na Creige Nuadh

The rain-speckled station sign. *Terry Gough*

The Borders Railway

Shawfair		68 C2
Opened	6 September 2015	
Operator	**original** ScotRail (Abellio)	

This is a new station serving a burgeoning residential area. It is located on a new alignment – not the original Waverley Route – at this point, as the latter was severed during the construction of the A720 City By-Pass road. Shawfair is served by a half-hourly Edinburgh-Tweedbank service, hourly on Sundays.

West Coast Railways No 37685 heads a Tweedbank-Edinburgh-Linlithgow excursion northbound through Shawfair on 18 August 2019. At the far end of the train is 'Black Five' steam loco No 44871. *Bob Avery*

Eskbank		57 B1
Previous names	Gallowshall, Eskbank & Dalkeith	
Opened	21 June 1847	
Closed (as Eskbank and Dalkeith)	6 January 1969	
Reopened	6 September 2015	
Operator	**original** NBR	

The station is approximately a third of a mile further south than the original, and exists primarily to serve the nearby towns of Dalkeith and Bonnyrigg. Car parking is available. The train service is as listed for Shawfair.

The 14.00 Tweedbank-Edinburgh service, formed by unit No 158704, arrives at Eskbank on 14 August 2019. *Bob Avery*

Above: A further view of the 14.00 Tweedbank-Edinburgh service, formed by unit No 158704, at Eskbank on 14 August 2019.

Left: The former 'Waverley Route' trackbed was used as a footpath and cycle way before reconstruction work started. This is the view near Eskbank, looking towards Edinburgh, on 10 July 2012. *Terry Gough*

Newtongrange		57 B1
Opened	1 August 1908	
Closed	6 January 1969	
Reopened	6 September 2015	
Operator	*original* NBR	

The new station is just short of a third of a mile further south than its predecessor. It serves the town of Newtongrange and the excellent Scottish National Mining Museum, which is nearby. Services are as shown for Shawfair.

A 10 July 2012 view of the trackbed of the Borders Railway at Newtongrange before the start of reconstruction. *Terry Gough*

The Borders Railway

No 158712, forming the 14.00 Tweedbank-Edinburgh service, pauses at Newtongrange on 23 July 2019. The bridge on the left of the first view carries the A7 Edinburgh-Carlisle trunk road. The pithead gear and chimney visible above the trees belong to the former Lady Victoria Colliery, now the superb Newtongrange mining museum. *Both Bob Avery*

Gorebridge		57 B1
Opened	14 July 1847	
Closed	6 January 1969	
Reopened	6 September 2015	
Operator	**original** NBR	

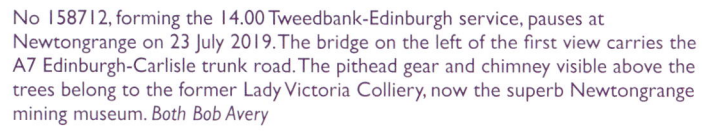

A single platform serves a popular small residential town. Services are as shown for Shawfair.

Above: In the very early days of the Borders Railway project, this is the site of Gorebridge station, looking south on 10 July 2012. *Terry Gough*

Right: No 158741, forming a Tweedbank-Edinburgh service, pulls away from Gorebridge on 14 August 2019. *Bob Avery*

Stow		57 B2
Opened	1 November 1848	
Closed	6 January 1969	
Reopened	6 September 2015	
P&P	No 9 p47	
Operator	*original* NBR	

For reasons that are not clear, Stow (pronounced as in 'cow') is only deemed worthy of an hourly service, and alternate Borders Railway trains do not call here, except on Sundays, when the route's hourly trains all make the call.

Above and left: Two views of the disused Stow station on 10 July 2012, prior to the commencement of reconstruction work, showing the former northbound-side waiting room and the surviving station building. *Both Terry Gough*

The 15.56 Tweedbank-Edinburgh service, formed of 'Turbostar' No 170414, calls at Stow on the same day. *Bob Avery*

The 15.24 Edinburgh-Tweedbank service calls at Stow on 14 August 2019. *Bob Avery*

The Borders Railway

On 10 September 2015 No 60009 *Union of South Africa* traverses the new Borders Railway near Stow. *Bob Avery*

Galashiels		57 C2
Opened	1 November 1849	
Closed	6 January 1969	
Reopened	6 September 2015	
P&P	No 9 p45	
Operator	**original** NBR	

The new station is slightly to the north of the original, and services are as shown for Shawfair.

A view of the site of the new Galashiels station on 10 July 2012, before reconstruction of the railway began. The original station was behind the road bridge in the background. *Terry Gough*

Passengers Once More

No 46100 *Royal Scot* leaves Galashiels with a special for Tweedbank on 4 September 2016. The 10mph speed restriction applies to traffic on a side road! *Bob Avery*

'A4' 'Pacific' No 60009 *Union of South Africa* pauses at Galashiels with the first of ScotRail's Edinburgh-Tweedbank Borders Railway steam trips on 10 September 2015. *Bob Avery*

Tweedbank		57 C2
Opened	6 September 2015	
Operator	**original** ScotRail (Abellio)	

This is the southern terminus of the Borders Railway from Edinburgh. It is linked to other nearby Borders towns by bus links and by a park and ride facility, though parking capacity is at times barely adequate, such has been the success of the project. It has an island platform with both faces capable of taking 12 coach locomotive hauled trains, which occasionally visit the line on charter services.

DB Cargo's No 67026 *Diamond Jubilee*, in its special livery, is about to head a return charter to Edinburgh from Tweedbank on 14 October 2015. *Bob Avery*

On the following day No 158782 departs from Tweedbank for Edinburgh. *Bob Avery*

OTHER EDINBURGH AND LOTHIANS STATIONS

Curriehill		57 A1
Previous name	Currie	
Opened	15 February 1848	
Closed	2 April 1951	
Reopened	5 October 1987	
Operator	original CR	

This station on the former Caledonian Railway route from Edinburgh Princes Street to the WCML at Carstairs was reopened to serve an expanding Edinburgh suburb. It is served by an hourly service between Edinburgh and Glasgow Central via Shotts, and one train each day to Glasgow Central via Carstairs and Motherwell, counterbalanced by one eastbound service running through Edinburgh to North Berwick. On Sundays the basic service is 2-hourly until around 19.00.

A Virgin 'Pendolino' working from Edinburgh to London Euston hurries through Curriehill on 4 July 2012. *Terry Gough*

At Curriehill the footbridge is attractively finished in a dark red and cream scheme. *Terry Gough*

The station sign. *Terry Gough*

South Gyle		57 A1
Opened	9 May 1985	
Operator	original BR	

This station serves the suburb of the same name, nearby office developments and the large Gyle Shopping Centre (though in practice Edinburgh Gateway and the Edinburgh Trams stop are closer). There are two tph to Haymarket and Edinburgh and two tph to the Fife Circle, alternate trains taking alternate directions around the circle. A limited peak-hour service operates to Tweedbank on weekdays.

The 12.08 Arbroath-Edinburgh service, formed of 'Turbostar' No 170406, passes South Gyle on 1 August 2019. *Bob Avery*

The 12.32 Cowdenbeath-Edinburgh service, this time 'Turbostar' No 170471, pulls into the station on the same day. *Bob Avery*

Other Edinburgh and Lothians stations

Edinburgh Gateway		57 A1
Opened	9 November 2016 (official); 11 November 2016 (services started)	
Operator	**original** ScotRail (Abellio)	

The completely new station was conceived as part of the Edinburgh to Glasgow Improvement Plan, which involved many improvements to rail services in central Scotland. It offers connections via escalators to the Edinburgh Trams route between the Airport and the City, thus offering airport access to passengers from the north without having to go to Edinburgh first. The station is served by four tph to Edinburgh. In the opposite direction there are two tph to Glenrothes (alternately via Dunfermline and Kirkcaldy), one tph to Dundee and Arbroath, and one tph to Perth. Trains to/from Aberdeen and Inverness do not call, though connections are available at Perth and Dundee. A slightly less frequent service operates on Sundays until approximately 19.30.

The 12.30 Edinburgh-Aberdeen service, formed of one of ScotRail's hand-me-down and refurbished HSTs, races through Edinburgh Gateway on 1 August 2019, the date of all these photographs. *Bob Avery*

The slightly late 11.03 Arbroath-Edinburgh service, formed of BTP-liveried No 170407 (right), passes No 158716 forming the 1235 Edinburgh-Perth service. *Bob Avery*

The escalator leading up from the tram stop to the main station. *Bob Avery*

The ticket hall at Edinburgh Gateway. The main line from Edinburgh to Aberdeen is out of picture on the left, while the Edinburgh Trams tracks can just be glimpsed through the glass, upper right. *Bob Avery*

Kingsknowe		68 C1
Previous name	King's Knowes	
Opened	15 February 1848	
Closed	6 July 1964	
Reopened	1 February 1971	
Operator	*original* CR	

This was another station opened by BR to serve the western suburbs of Edinburgh. Train services are as shown for Curriehill. An automatic half-barrier level crossing lay at the platform's western end, requiring the drivers of westbound trains calling here to press a plunger to start the barrier sequence. This has now been converted to full barriers controlled by CCTV, which obviates that requirement.

A Virgin Trains Euston-Birmingham-Edinburgh 'Pendolino' descends towards the Scottish capital through Kingsknowe on 14 August 2019. *Bob Avery*

Other Edinburgh and Lothians stations

Livingston South		56 B2
Opened	6 October 1984	
Operator	original BR	

This is a new station to serve the new town of Livingston, on the former Caledonian Railway Edinburgh Princes Street to Glasgow Central route via Shotts. Livingston also has another station, Livingston North, listed elsewhere. There are two tph to Edinburgh, and two tph to Glasgow Central, alternate trains operating to a limited-stop schedule. A reduced frequency operates on Sundays. At the time of writing electrification is complete and electric services have commenced.

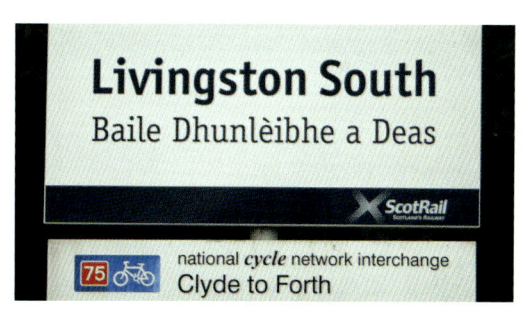

The station sign. *Terry Gough*

GBRf's No 66739 heads west through Livingston South on 30 July 2019 with the thrice-weekly Blyth-Fort William alumina tanks. *Bob Avery*

The raised nature of Livingston South station is illustrated here on the same day. A Class 385 from Glasgow Central to Edinburgh is arriving. *Bob Avery*

Wester Hailes		57 A1
Opened	11 May 1987	
Operator	**original** BRB	

Another station opened to serve a new suburb to the west of Edinburgh. Train services are as shown for Curriehill.

In cloudburst conditions, No 156508 calls at Wester Hailes with an Edinburgh-bound Shotts line service on 4 July 2012. Since recent electrification, these services are now provided by new Hitachi Class 385 EMUs. *Terry Gough*

The 08.10 Manchester Airport-Edinburgh service, formed of a TPE Class 350 EMU, passes Wester Hailes on 14 August 2019. *Bob Avery*

Other Edinburgh and Lothians stations

Musselburgh		68 C2
Opened	3 October 1988	
Operator	**original** BR	

This is a new station built to serve an important suburb of eastern Edinburgh. The original NBR Musselburgh station was located some distance away on the former Edinburgh & Dalkeith Railway line to Fisherrow, and closed in 1964. There is a basic hourly service each way between Edinburgh and North Berwick (including Sundays), increasing to half-hourly on Saturdays. In addition there is a limited service between Edinburgh and Dunbar, and occasional westbound services carry on to Haymarket, Glasgow Central and Ayr (not Sundays).

Above A brand-new LNER 'Azuma' train on a crew-training run speeds south through Musselburgh on 14 August 2019. *Bob Avery*

Right: Minutes away from the end of its journey from London, a northbound LNER Edinburgh-bound express streaks through Musselburgh on the same day. *Bob Avery*

Above: The station sign, photographed on 8 July 2012. *Terry Gough*

Left: Edinburgh-North Berwick services, formed of the now ubiquitous Hitachi Class 385s, pass at Musselburgh. *Bob Avery*

Passengers Once More

Wallyford		57 A2
Opened	June 1886	
Closed	October 1867	
Reopened	13 June 1994	
Operator	*original* NBR	

The original station had a pitifully short life, and the current station was opened under Railtrack auspices. Train services are as shown for Musselburgh. The station is marketed as having Park & Ride facilities, and there is a frequent bus service to the city as well as the trains. Ample car parking is available.

Above: A southbound HST, probably an Aberdeen-King's Cross service, hurries south on the ECML through Wallyford on 8 July 2012, the date of these three views. *Terry Gough*

Right: A Class 91, in its silver 'East Coast' livery, propels its Edinburgh-King's Cross express at speed through Wallyford. *Terry Gough*

Other Edinburgh and Lothians stations

With the Pentland Hills in the distance, a Class 380 unit forms a service from North Berwick leaving Wallyford on its journey along the ECML into Edinburgh. *Terry Gough*

Meadowbank		(68 C2)
Opened	14 June 1986	
Closed	20 March 1988	
Operator	**original** BR	

This station was built specifically to convey spectators going to Meadowbank stadium in eastern Edinburgh, in particular for the 1986 Commonwealth Games, when a shuttle service ran from Edinburgh Waverley station. It was also used for occasional events until 1988, when it closed. It is located on the branch line to Edinburgh's Powderhall refuse terminal, formerly an NBR branch to Leith. The branch itself is currently mothballed following the cessation of freight traffic, and little trace of the station is visible.

The site of the former Meadowbank stadium station, looking east on 5 July 2012. *Terry Gough*

Winchburgh Junction to Dalmeny Junction line   57 A1

This route links the former NBR main line from Edinburgh to Glasgow to the line from Edinburgh to Fife via the Forth Bridge. It lost its passenger service on 1 January 1973, but regained a peak-hour Glasgow-Kirkcaldy-and-return service in June 1996. In the intervening period it survived on freights between Mossend yard and destinations in Fife, and particularly coal trains to Longannet power station, which were rerouted in 2008 (and have subsequently ceased altogether).

None other than the famous *Flying Scotsman* lifts an SRPS Forth Circle special off the Winchburgh-Dalmeny line at Dalmeny Junction on 19 May 2019. *Steven Mackay*

BO'NESS & KINNEIL RAILWAY

Bo'ness (Bo'ness & Kinneil Railway)		56 A2
Opened	10 June 1856	
Closed	7 May 1956	
Reopened	1985	
Operator	original NBR	

Bo'ness is the main station of the Bo'ness & Kinneil heritage railway, near Linlithgow, operated by the Scottish Railway Preservation Society. Bo'ness is short for Borrowstounness, but the abbreviated version is universally used. The original station was about a quarter of a mile west of the present one, which is of new construction, but has a trainshed from Haymarket, a station building from Wormit in Fife, a footbridge from Murthly, north of Perth, and a Caledonian Railway signal box from Garnqueen South Junction near Coatbridge. All buildings as a group are Grade A listed structures. The excellent Museum of Scottish Railways is next door. The railway operates on weekends and most Tuesdays between late March and the end of October, and daily in August.

Bo'ness station sign and signal box, photographed on 2 January 2016. *Bob Avery*

Visiting Furness Railway No 20 is seen at Bo'ness during a gala event on 25 October 2015. *Bob Avery*

Below: Visiting GWR 0-6-2T No 5643 shunts the resident Caledonian Railway coaches at Bo'ness during a gala event on 21 October 2017. *Bob Avery*

Kinneil (Bo'ness & Kinneil Railway)		56 A2
Opened	1 January 1899	
Closed	(1) 1 January 1917, (2) 22 September 1930	
Reopened	(1) 1 September 1919, (2) 1985	
Operator	original NBR	

The first station from Bo'ness, 7 minutes ride away by train, this is a good kicking-off point for walks along the southern bank of the Firth of Forth. There are no facilities other than a single platform.

Kinneil Halt, Bo'ness & Kinneil Railway, photographed on 4 July 2012. *Terry Gough*

Visiting Gresley condensing 'N2' Class 0-6-2T No 1744 nears Kinneil with the 10.45 Bo'ness-Manuel service on 28 October 2013. *Bob Avery*

Birkhill (Bo'ness & Kinneil Railway)		56 A2
Opened	1989	
Operator	original SRPS (line was NBR).	

This new station, opened by the Scottish Railway Preservation Society, serves the adjacent Birkhill Fireclay Mine. The station building has parts from a building at Monifieth (near Dundee), and was exhibited at the Glasgow Garden Festival before being moved to Birkhill. The station's track layout is in the process of being fully signalled, which will increase the line capacity.

Caledonian Railway 0-4-4T No 419 has run round its train and will shortly return to Bo'ness on 4 January 2009. *Bob Avery*

Below: The same loco heads ex-LNER 4-4-0 No 246 *Morayshire* at Birkhill on the same day. *Bob Avery*

Top left and above: Caledonian Railway 0-4-4T No 55189 in its BR guise is employed on a photo charter at Birkhill on 1 March 2009. *Both Bob Avery*

Manuel (Bo'ness & Kinneil Railway)		56 A2
Previous name	Bo'ness Junction	
Opened	21 February 1842	
Closed	6 March 1967	
Reopened	29 June 2013	
Operator	**original** NBR	

Originally Bo'ness Junction on the main Edinburgh-Glasgow route, this station is now the end of the Bo'ness & Kinneil heritage line. There's no public access but this may happen in future years. An east-facing connection with the main line exists to allow movements to and from the National Network. The station area has a complex history including former Manuel High Level and Low Level stations.

Former NCB 'Austerity' tank No 7 (bearing its WD number 75254) runs round its train at Manuel on the Bo'ness & Kinneil Railway on 4 July 2012, as a 'Turbostar' rushes past on its Glasgow Queen Street to Edinburgh journey. This scene has since been transformed by electrification of the main line, and the construction of a platform (only accessible to B&KR train passengers). *Terry Gough*

GREATER GLASGOW STATIONS

Argyle Line

The following seven stations form Glasgow's Argyle Line, opened in 1979, linking former sections of suburban railway that had succumbed to the Beeching Axe in 1964. The line runs from a new grade-separated junction with the North Clyde Airdrie-Helensburgh line near Finnieston, via a largely subterranean route through the City Centre (more or less under the city's east-west Argyle Street), to a junction with the WCML at Rutherglen Central Junction. The term 'Argyle Line' is also used loosely to refer to the group of electric suburban services that use the new line – mainly to Dalmuir and Milngavie to the north-west and to Motherwell, Whifflet and Larkhall to the south-east. The whole line was closed for nine months between Christmas 1994 and September 1995 due to flood damage, necessitating diversion of trains from Lanarkshire via Whifflet and Queen Street Low Level. The current service pattern is:

Mondays to Saturdays

- 2 tph to Dalmuir via Yoker
- 2 tph to Dalmuir via Singer
- 2 tph to Milngavie via Westerton
- 2 tph to Whifflet, with an hourly extension to Motherwell
- 2 tph to Larkhall via Hamilton
- 1 tph to Motherwell via Hamilton
- 1 tph to Cumbernauld via Hamilton and Motherwell

Sundays

- 2 tph to Balloch via Yoker
- 2 tph to Milngavie
- 1 tph to Larkhall
- 1 tph to Motherwell via Whifflet
- 2 tph to Motherwell via Hamilton

Anderston		104 B1
Previous name	Anderston Cross	
Opened	10 August 1896	
Closed	3 August 1959.	
Reopened	5 November 1979.	
Operator	original CR	

The station serves a financial district, several hotels, and nearby residential areas. It has restricted opening hours on Sundays, between 10.00 and 18.00 only. Some peak-hour services terminate or start their journeys here, utilising the turnback siding adjacent to (but not part of) Exhibition Centre station.

A Dalmuir-Motherwell via Whifflet service formed of unit No 320304 runs in to the semi-subterranean Anderston station on 22 May 2019. *Bob Avery*

Argyle Line

Exhibition Centre		104 B1
Previous names	Stobcross, Finnieston	
Opened	1 May 1896	
Closed	**(as Stobcross)**	3 August 1959
Reopened (as Finnieston)	5 November 1979; name changed to Exhibition Centre in 1986	
Operator	**original** CR	

The station is linked to the Scottish Event Campus (formerly Exhibition and Conference Centre) and also the SSE Hydro and SEC Armadillo, both major concert venues, by a covered footbridge from just outside the station entrance. Patronage is considerable from people attending exhibitions, events and concerts, and pedestrian congestion can be a problem at times.

Top right: No 47484 *Isambard Kingdom Brunel* makes a rare appearance at Exhibition Centre on 3 June 1988 with a loco-hauled special from Aberdeen. This unusual destination was to allow passengers to visit Glasgow's Garden Festival. *Bob Avery*

Right: Preserved Class 40 No 40145 heads the SRPS Carlisle-Fort William railtour, approaching Exhibition Centre station on Glasgow's normally EMU-only Argyle Line, on 25 August 2007. This is believed to be the first ever working of a 40-hauled passenger train through the Argyle Line (and was certainly the first visit of a Class 40 to the West Highland Line). *Bob Avery*

Below: No 320403 emerges from Stobcross Street Tunnel into daylight at Exhibition Centre, bound for Dalmuir on 22 May 2019. *Bob Avery*

Bottom right: On the same day No 320320 emerges from Kelvinhaugh Tunnel (which forms part of the burrowing junction for up Argyle Line trains heading east from Partick) into brief daylight at Exhibition Centre. *Bob Avery*

Glasgow Central Low Level		104 B1
Opened	10 August 1896	
Closed	3 October 1964	
Reopened	5 November 1979	
Operator	original CR	

Originally part of a Caledonian Railway route from Maryhill, the line through the subterranean Low Level station fell to the Beeching Axe until reopened as part of the Argyle Line project. Managed separately from the main-line station (by ScotRail rather than Network Rail), it consists of a single island platform. Another disused island platform lies hidden behind tunnel walls to the north of the running lines.

Above: No 320424 runs into Platform 17 (the two underground platforms are numbered 16 and 17 following on from the main station's 15 platforms) with a westbound service on 22 May 2019. *Bob Avery*

Left: These are the low level platforms looking west, as an eastbound train calls on 25 July 2019. *Bob Avery*

Argyle Street		104 B1
Opened	5 November 1979	
Operator	original BR	

This brand-new station was built as part of the Argyle Line project. Its subterranean island platform is located below its namesake street in one of Glasgow's main shopping areas, with easy access on foot to various parts of the city.

A westbound train pauses at Argyle Street on 22 May 2019 while an eastbound Class 318 is about to emerge from the tunnel leading to Glasgow Central Low Level. *Bob Avery*

Argyle Line

Another view of the westbound six-car unit, pausing at the subterranean station. *Bob Avery*

Bridgeton		104 B1
Opened	1 November 1895.	
Closed	5 October 1964	
Reopened	5 November 1979	
Operator	**original** CR	

The station was originally a junction for a direct line to Carmyle, but only the original Rutherglen line platforms were reopened. The station serves Glasgow Green and extensive residential districts nearby. It is not to be confused with the nearby Bridgeton Central station, which closed in November 1979 when the Argyle Line reopened, and served as an EMU depot until June 1987.

No 318265 runs into Bridgeton forming a westbound Argyle Line service on 22 May 2019. *Bob Avery*

This external view of Bridgeton on the same day shows the famous bandstand. The Argyle Line runs under the street across the picture. *Bob Avery*

Dalmarnock		104 B1
Opened	1 November 1895, replacing a station at a higher level	
Closed	5 October 1964	
Reopened	5 November 1979	
Operator	**original** CR	

This station lies half in and half out of the Argyle Line's tunnels. It serves residential areas, many industrial units and Celtic's Parkhead football stadium. Other sporting venues are nearby and the station received a makeover in time for the 2014 Commonwealth Games, necessitating closure from 4 June 2012 until the spring of the following year; this was an overrun of six months due to groundwork issues.

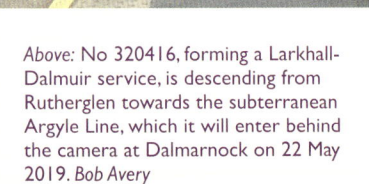

Above: No 320416, forming a Larkhall-Dalmuir service, is descending from Rutherglen towards the subterranean Argyle Line, which it will enter behind the camera at Dalmarnock on 22 May 2019. *Bob Avery*

Left: Overhead concrete beams cast shadows onto the platform as a Class 320 passes en route from Larkhall to Dalmuir. *Bob Avery*

Argyle Line

Rutherglen		104 C1
Opened	31 March 1879	
Closed	5 October 1964	
Reopened	6 May 1974 (WCML platforms), 5 November 1979 (Argyle Line platforms)	
Operator	**original** CR	

The Beeching Axe fell on the original Glasgow Central Railway in 1964, but an island platform on the adjacent slow lines of the WCML opened ten years later, served by a new electric service from Motherwell and Hamilton to Glasgow Central. These platforms closed when the Argyle Line opened in 1979, following the original CR formation. The new M74 motorway now covers the northern end of the curved island platform

A Class 334, forming an eastbound Argyle Line service, is about to curve left and join the WCML tracks, visible in the background. *Bob Avery*

Looking towards Dalmarnock and Glasgow on 22 May 2019, the date of these three pictures, a Class 320 is departing from Rutherglen as the 11.33 Larkhall-Milngavie service. Overhead is the M74 extension viaduct (opened in June 2011), which unintentionally serves to shelter waiting passengers from not infrequent rain. *Bob Avery*

A six-car Class 320 formation curves into Rutherglen's down platform from the WCML. *Bob Avery*

Paisley Canal line

The original Paisley Canal line formed a loop off the main Glasgow to Ayr route. It takes its name from the canal acquired by the Glasgow & South Western Railway in 1865 and converted into a railway. It left the main line at Shields Junction and rejoined at Elderslie, continuing to Kilmacolm. It was built initially to ease congestion on the direct line via Paisley Gilmour Street, and frequently proved its worth as a diversionary route. Passenger services to Kilmacolm ceased in 1983. The present service to Paisley Canal was introduced just seven years later in 1990, involving reopening five stations and one brand-new one, listed below. There is a half-hourly service to Glasgow on Monday-Saturday, with an hourly service on Sundays. The reopened line is single track with a 'dynamic loop' situated between Crookston and Mosspark. The line was electrified in 2012.

Paisley Canal		103 B1
Opened	1 July 1885	
Closed	10 January 1983	
Reopened	28 July 1990	
Operator	original G&SWR	

The new station is situated on the east side of Causeyside Street, the opposite side from the original G&SWR facility.

Soon-to-be-withdrawn unit No 314216, wearing its carmine and cream Strathclyde PTE livery till the end, stands at Paisley Canal on 29 April 2019, about to form the 16.05 service to Glasgow Central. *Bob Avery*

'Deltic' No 55022 calls at Paisley Canal during the SRPS 'Routes and Branches' tour of 24 August 2008. Class 40 No 40145 is at the other end. *Bob Avery*

Paisley Canal Line 87

Hawkhead		103 B1
Opened	1 May 1894	
Closed	14 February 1966	
Reopened	12 April 1991	
Operator	original G&SWR	

The station was closed between 1917 and 1919 due to the First World War.

No 318267 forming the 13.42 Glasgow-Central-Paisley Canal service leaves Hawkhead, the penultimate station on the branch, on 18 July 2019. In the background is Paisley's Abbey Mill, a Victorian industrial building converted into offices. *Bob Avery*

Crookston		103 B2
Opened	1 July 1885	
Closed	10 January 1983	
Reopened	28 July 1990	
Operator	original G&SWR	

Like Hawkhead, it was closed for two years from 1 January 1917 due to World War 1.

Above: No 380009 calls at Crookston was the 13.12 Glasgow Central-Paisley Canal service on 18 July 2019. *Bob Avery*

Left: Looking towards Glasgow on the same day, on the left is the former station building, tastefully converted into private dwellings. Beyond the bridge is the start of the 'dynamic loop' (i.e. a short double-track section) between Crookston and Mosspark, which enables a half-hourly service to operate on the Paisley Canal branch. *Bob Avery*

Mosspark		103 B2
Previous name	Mosspark West	
Opened	1 March 1934	
Closed	10 January 1983	
Reopened	28 July 1990	
Operator	original LMS	

The station was opened by the LMS in 1934 to serve residential developments. The 'West' suffix was dropped in May 1974; there was never a Mosspark East.

Above: A Paisley Canal-Glasgow Central service draws into Mosspark. *Bob Avery*

Above: Looking north-east towards Glasgow on 25 July 2019, the date of these three views, Mosspark station is seen from a public footbridge that crosses the station. *Bob Avery*

Below: The 16.42 Glasgow Central to Paisley Canal service approaches Mosspark. *Bob Avery*

Paisley Canal Line   89

Corkerhill		103 B2
Previous name	Corkerhill Halt (14 July 1924 until closure)	
Opened	1 December 1896	
Closed	10 January 1983	
Reopened	28 July 1990	
Operator	*original* G&SWR	

The station is in fairly close proximity to ScotRail's maintenance depot nearby.

Top left: In pre-electrification days, and before the station's 1983 closure, a Cravens power car leads a three-car DMU into Corkerhill, heading towards Glasgow – a date in the early 1970s seems probable. Overhead electrification, rationalisation and tree growth have since transformed this scene. *The late Willy McKnight*

Above: The east end of Corkerhill station is seen on 16 July 2019, the date of the next three pictures. The track through the disused former down platform is a headshunt to facilitate moves at the west end of ScotRail's Corkerhill depot, situated out of sight around the corner. The large mirror is an aid to driver's visibility on the curved platform. *Bob Avery*

Top right: The 15.35 Paisley Canal to Glasgow Central service runs into Corkerhill, with the disused former down platform headshunt line on the left. *Bob Avery*

Above: The 15.42 Glasgow Central-Paisley Canal service draws into the station. The sign on the disused platform acknowledges the completion of the relatively recent electrification. *Bob Avery*

Dumbreck		103 B2
Opened	28 July 1990	
Operator	original ScotRail (National Express)	

The station is a new one, though close to the site of the former Bellahouston station, which closed in 1954. It serves a residential area and also Glasgow's Bellahouston Park, a large area of rich parkland and the venue for many outdoor events.

Classes 320 (left) and 380 pass at Dunbreck on Paisley Canal workings on 16 July 2019. No 320315 is about to pass under the M77 motorway on its run towards Shields Junction and Glasgow.
Bob Avery

Rutherglen East Junction to Whifflet

This stretch of line, with five intermediate stations listed below, regained its passenger service in 1993. It had succumbed to the Beeching Axe in October 1964, surviving on freight trains (primarily to the huge Ravenscraig steelworks near Motherwell) and occasional diversions. In the 1980s there were plans to shut it completely – freight could be rerouted and the line had achieved notoriety for vandal attacks on trains, infrastructure and crews. However, a pro-rail Strathclyde PTE supported reopening, and a new half-hourly diesel service between Glasgow Central and Whifflet commenced in October 1993. Electrification was completed in 2014, and Whifflet line services were incorporated into Glasgow's Argyle Line service pattern, greatly improving journey opportunities.

The service pattern comprises two tph to Dalmuir and two tph to Whifflet, alternate trains continuing to Motherwell. On Sundays there is an hourly service each way between Motherwell and Balloch until around 19.00.

Carmyle		104 C2
Opened	18 January 1866	
Closed	5 October 1964	
Reopened	4 October 1993	
Operator	original CR	

Rutherglen East Junction to Whifflet

Eastbound and westbound trains pass at Carmyle on 16 July 2019. The eastbound train (in the distance) is about to pass under the M74 motorway. *Bob Avery*

A late-morning Dalmuir-Whifflet service formed of unit No 318255 and a sibling enters the station on the same day. *Bob Avery*

Mount Vernon		104 B2
Opened	8 January 1866	
Closed	16 August 1943	
Reopened	4 October 1993	
Operator	*original* CR	

A ticket machine waits for its next customer at Mount Vernon as a Class 320 unit runs in forming a Motherwell-Dalmuir working on 16 July 2019. *Bob Avery*

A six-car Class 320/318 combination pulls away from Mount Vernon towards Whifflet on the same day. *Bob Avery*

Baillieston			104 B2
Opened	8 January 1866		
Closed	5 October 1964		
Reopened	4 October 1993		
Operator	original CR		

A six-car Class 320 formation arrives at Baillieston forming a Dalmuir-Motherwell working on 16 July 2019. *Bob Avery*

Another six-car Class 320 formation heads east from Baillieston towards Whifflet on the same day. *Bob Avery*

Bargeddie			104 B2
Previous name	Drumpark		
Opened	Not recorded		
Closed	5 October 1964		
Reopened	4 October 1993		
Operator	original LMS		

The new station at Bargeddie is reported to be on the site of the former Drumpark station; however, little information exists.

No 320404 and a stablemate run into Bargeddie with a Whifflet-Dalmuir working on 16 July 2019, the date of these three views. *Bob Avery*

Greater Glasgow stations

Below: A six-car Class 320/318 hybrid accelerates westbound from Bargeddie with a Motherwell-Dalmuir working. *Bob Avery*

Right: With the station lights burning for no apparent reason, a single Class 318 unit approaches forming a Dalmuir-Whifflet service. *Bob Avery*

Kirkwood		56 C1
Opened	4 October 1993	
Operator	**original** ScotRail (National Express)	

Kirkwood serves the eastern end of the town of Coatbridge.

Unit No 334013 approaches Kirkwood as the 12.25 Motherwell-Dalmuir service on 16 July 2019. *Bob Avery*

No 320417 brings up the rear of the 11.35 Dalmuir-Whifflet service, seen at Kirkwood on the same day. *Bob Avery*

Glasgow Queen Street to Anniesland

This new service from Glasgow was started in 1993 calling at five new or reopened stations, listed below. In 2005 it was extended in a south-westerly direction via Kelvindale to Anniesland, though there was no physical connection with the existing North Clyde line there until one was provided in 2015 to facilitate diversions in connection with the redevelopment of Queen Street station. There is a half-hourly service in each direction, hourly on Sundays (until 19.00), between Queen Street and Anniesland.

Ashfield		104 B1
Opened	6 December 1993	
Operator	**original** BR	

No 66739 with the thrice-weekly Blyth-Fort William bulk alumina train – known to railwayman as 'the bulks' – passes Ashfield on 16 July 2019. *Bob Avery*

Glasgow Queen Street to Anniesland

Possilpark & Parkhouse		104 B1
Previous name	Possilpark	
Opened	1 February 1885	
Closed	1 January 1917	
Reopened	6 December 1993	
Operator	original NBR	

The new station is located a short distance to the east of the earlier one.

Above: A Glasgow Queen Street to Anniesland service calls 15 May 2019. *Bob Avery*

Left: 'B1' 4-6-0 No 61306 *Mayflower* drifts through Possilpark & Parkhouse en route from Fort William to Penrith with the 'Highlands and Islands' railtour on 15 May 2019. *Bob Avery*

Gilshochill		104 A1
Previous name	Lambhill	
Opened	6 December 1993	
Operator	original BR	

The station was renamed Gilshochill (pronounced Gilsie-hill) on 24 May 1998.

Right: Steps lead to the up and down platforms at Gilshochill; as yet there is no ramped access. *Bob Avery*

Left: No 158720 forms an afternoon Glasgow Queen Street to Anniesland service on 19 May 2019. *Bob Avery*

Passengers Once More

Summerston		104 A1
Opened	6 December 1993	
Operator	**original** BR	

The original Summerston station, closed in 1951, was on the erstwhile Kelvin Valley Railway between Maryhill and Kilsyth.

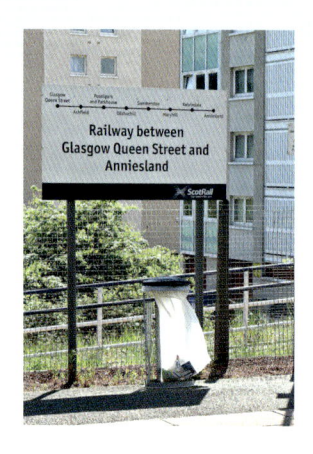

Above and centre: No 158739, forming a Glasgow Queen Street to Anniesland service, arrives at Summerston on 15 May 2019. *Both Bob Avery*

Sign and waste bin at Summerston. *Bob Avery*

Maryhill		103 A2
Previous name	Maryhill Park	
Opened	28 May 1858	
Closed	2 April 1951	
Reopened	19 December 1960	
Closed	2 March 1964 (restricted service only from 2 October 1961)	
Reopened	6 December 1993	
Operator	**original** NBR	

This station has a complex history with contradictory references. It bore the name 'Maryhill Park' for less than a year between 1960 and 1961.

GBRf's No 66738 heads the thrice-weekly Fort William-Blyth alumina empties through Maryhill on 15 May 2019. *Bob Avery*

Greater Glasgow stations

An Anniesland-Glasgow Queen Street service comes off the Anniesland line at Maryhill Park Junction and arrives at Maryhill station, also on 15 May 2019. *Both Bob Avery*

An Anniesland-Glasgow Queen street service pulls into Maryhill. 15th May 2019. *Bob Avery*

Kelvindale		103 A2
Opened	26 September 2005	
Operator	**original** First ScotRail	

Left: No 158711 arrives at the new station on the same day. It carries the National Express livery. *Bob Avery*

Right: No 158735, forming an Anniesland-Queen Street working, arrives at the new station at Kelvindale on its opening day, 26 September 2005. The new station is the only intermediate station on the new line extending Queen Street-Maryhill services to Anniesland. *Bob Avery*

Left: Another opening day view, this time of No 158723, also in National Express livery, on an Anniesland-Glasgow Queen Street working. *Bob Avery*

Larkhall line

The new line from Haughead Junction near Hamilton to the town of Larkhall, opened in 2005, was the first new railway in Scotland since the opening of Glasgow's Argyle Line (featured elsewhere) in 1979. Three new stations feature, listed below. The new line was widely misreported on opening as a new line all the way to Milngavie. The branch from Maryhill to Anniesland via Kelvindale (listed earlier), though not physically connected, was an important part of the Larkhall plans as it vacated paths (previously used by empty stock trains) on the north side of Glasgow to allow Larkhall services to run. The new line enjoys a half-hourly weekday service to Milngavie via the Argyle Line, with an hourly service to Balloch on Sundays. There is speculation about extending the line further south to the Lanarkshire towns of Stonehouse and Strathaven.

Chatelherault		56 B1
Previous name	Ferniegair	
Opened	2 October 1876	
Closed	1 January 1917	
Reopened	9 December 2005	
Operator	original CR	

This station (pronounced 'Shattler Row') serves the booming residential district of Ferniegair and is named after the Duke of Hamilton's estate, part of which is now a nearby country park. The single-platform station has ample car parking.

Above: The street-level entrance to Chatelherault station. *Bob Avery*

Right: Class 334s have a few diagrams on Argyle Line services, permeating the usual diet of Classes 318 and 320. Here unit No 334020 runs into Chatelherault forming a Larkhall to Dalmuir service on 25 March 2019. *Bob Avery*

Larkhall Line

Merryton		56 B1
Opened	9 December 2005.	
Operator	**original** First ScotRail	

This single platform serves a residential area, with good parking facilities.

A six-car paired Class 320 formation on a Dalmuir-Larkhall working arrives at Merryton on 25 March 2019. The second view shows the footpath and other paraphernalia on the approach to the station's single platform. *Both Bob Avery*

Larkhall		56 B1
Previous name	Larkhall Central	
Opened	1 July 1905	
Closed	4 October 1965	
Reopened	9 December 2005	
Operator	**original** CR	

The station enjoys a good town centre location, but only limited street parking is available.

Unit No 334021 has just arrived at Larkhall on 9 December 2005, the opening day of the new station, to be greeted by a local pipe band. The opening ceremony is about to take place, carried out by Scotland's First Minister, Right Hon Jack McConnell MSP. Full train services commenced on 13 December. *Bob Avery*

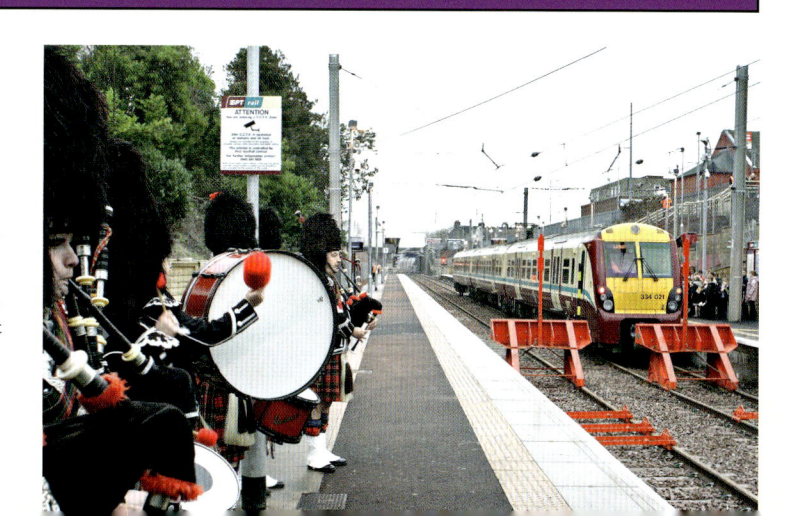

Above left: No 334021 stands at the brand-new Larkhall station on the opening day, shortly to depart for Glasgow with VIPs and invited guests after the opening ceremony. *Bob Avery*

Above Excited schoolchildren wave their flags at Scotland's First Minister, Jack McConnell MSP. *Bob Avery*

Left: No 334021 *Larkhall* prepares to leave for Glasgow. *Bob Avery*

Below: On 24 July 2007 Nos 37605/06 head Network Rail's Overhead Line Mentor test coach at the normally EMU-only Larkhall station. *Bob Avery*

OTHER GREATER GLASGOW STATIONS

Airbles		56, B1
Opened	15 May 1989	
Operator	**original** BR	

This station was opened under BR auspices to serve the southern part of Lanarkshire, in particular the nearby Motherwell College and Civic Centre, and Motherwell Football Club's Fir Park ground. It is located on the Hamilton Circle Route between Motherwell and Hamilton.

The basic weekday service is four tph, comprising two tph from Milngavie to Motherwell, alternate trains carrying on to Cumbernauld via Coatbridge Central. In the opposite direction are two tph (one of which originates at Cumbernauld) to Dalmuir via Hamilton and Glasgow's Argyle Line. Service frequency is similar on Sundays but there are no through services to Cumbernauld.

The station sign. *Bob Avery*

Airbles station, looking down the ramp onto Platform 2 (for Motherwell) on 30 July 2019. *Bob Avery*

Two six-car Class 320 formations pass at Airbles, also on 30 July 2019. *Bob Avery*

Branchton		55 A1
Opened	5 June 1967	
Operator	**original** BR	

Branchton enjoys a daily hourly service in each direction to Glasgow Central and Wemyss Bay.

Above: Branchton, looking towards Wemyss Bay on 10 June 2012. *Terry Gough*

Left: The station buildings at Branchton, showing easy interchange between rail and bus. *Terry Gough*

Other Greater Glasgow stations

Drumfrochar		55 A1
Opened	24 May 1998	
Operator	original BR	

The train service is as shown for Branchton.

Right: Drumfrochar, looking north-east towards Glasgow on 10 June 2012. *Terry Gough*

Below: A Wemyss Bay to Glasgow Central service formed of unit No 380111 calls at Drumfrochar on the same day. *Terry Gough*

Drumry		103 A2
Opened	6 April 1953	
Operator	**original** BR	

Located on the North Clyde Line via Singer, Drumry enjoys two tph to Airdrie, two tph to Larkhall, two tph to Balloch and two tph to Dalmuir. On Sundays, a half-hourly Edinburgh-Helensburgh Central service calls in each direction.

Above: Up and down Class 320 units on Dalmuir-Larkhall services pass at Drumry, on 18 July 2019. *Bob Avery*

Right: A fast service for Helensburgh, formed by unit No 334008, passes Drumry also on 18 July 2019. *Bob Avery*

Other Greater Glasgow stations

Garscadden		103 B2
Opened	5 November 1960	
Operator	original BR	

This station is on Glasgow's North Clyde network. It has an island platform, and enjoys two tph to Whifflet (alternate trains carry on to Motherwell), two tph to Springburn, two tph to Dumbarton Central and two tph to Dalmuir. On Sundays there is one tph to Motherwell via Whifflet, one tph to Larkhall, and two tph to Balloch. The station is close to ScotRail's Yoker depot so some peak-hour trains start and terminate here as the first/last stop after/before the depot.

Right: With the Titan Crane at Clydebank (now a tourist attraction) just visible in the distance, a westbound Class 334 accelerates away from Garscadden on 25 July 2019. The unit is approaching the connection to ScotRail's Yoker depot, out of sight on the left behind the unit.
Bob Avery

Left: A Dalmuir-bound Class 320 approaches Garscadden from the east on the same day. The 'locomotive' plant pot is a feature found on many Scottish stations.
Bob Avery

Passengers Once More

Gartcosh		56 A1
Opened	1 June 1831	
Closed	5 November 1962	
Reopened	9 May 2005	
Operator	original CR	

Following recent electrification, a half-hourly service between Glasgow Queen Street and Edinburgh via Falkirk Grahamston serves Gartcosh. On Sundays an hourly service operates between Glasgow and Cumbernauld.

Left: The 11.23 Glasgow Queen Street-Falkirk Grahamston service calls at Gartcosh on the opening day, 9 May 2005. Children from Gartcosh Primary and other invited guests pose for photos. The station was officially opened by HRH Princess Anne a few weeks earlier, but the actual opening was delayed until 9 May due to power supply problems. *Bob Avery*

Below: Strathclyde-liveried 'Turbostar' Class 170s on Cumbernauld and Falkirk Grahamston services pass at the new station at Gartcosh on its opening day. This line was subsequently electrified. *Bob Avery*

Bottom left Brand-new Hitachi Class 385 EMU No 385113 calls at Gartcosh on a Glasgow Queen Street to Edinburgh via Falkirk Grahamston working on 30 March 2019. *Bob Avery*

Other Greater Glasgow stations

Greenfaulds		56 A1
Opened	15 May 1989	
Operator	**original** BR	

Greenfaulds is located in the western part of Cumbernauld and has excellent Park & Ride facilities. It enjoys a frequent Monday to Saturday train service – two tph in each direction between Glasgow Queen Street and Edinburgh via Falkirk Grahamston, and one tph each way between Dalmuir (via Motherwell) and Cumbernauld. An hourly Sunday service operates between Glasgow Queen Street and Cumbernauld.

Right: DB Cargo's No 66021 heads Grangemouth-Daventry containers through Greenfaulds on 30 March 2019, the date of all these views. *Bob Avery*

The path down to the platform on the down side, seen as a Class 318 formation calls forming a Glasgow-Cumbernauld via Motherwell service. *Bob Avery*

Unit No 380002 calls at Greenfaulds while working a Glasgow Queen Street to Edinburgh service via Cumbernauld and Falkirk Grahamston. *Bob Avery*

Howwood		55 B2
Previous name	Howood	
Opened	21 July 1840	
Closed	11 August 1840	
Reopened	1 December 1876	
Closed	7 March 1955	
Reopened	12 March 2005	
Operator	original G&SWR	

Howwood enjoys a half-hourly service between Glasgow Central and Ayr, with some additional services to/from Ardrossan Harbour. On Sundays this becomes an hourly service, with westbound trains heading for Largs.

Local enterprise provides embellishments to Howwood station, looking towards Glasgow on 29 April 2019. *Bob Avery*

Station Road, Howwood. *Bob Avery*

An Ayr-Glasgow Central express formed by the usual Class 380 EMU speeds through Howood on 29 April 2012. *Bob Avery*

Other Greater Glasgow stations

Hyndland		103 B2
Opened	15 March 1886	
Closed	5 November 1960	
Reopened	5 November 1960 (on new site)	
P&P	No 31 p78	
Operator	original NBR	

The original NBR station was at the end of a short branch from Partickhill, but was replaced by the current station upon electrification of the line in 1960. The original station survived for a short spell as an EMU maintenance depot, which lasted until 1987. Little trace remains today.

Hyndland enjoys an intensive service with all trains on the Glasgow North Clyde and Argyle lines calling here. It serves a substantial residential area, the Gartnavel General Hospital and two other hospitals nearby.

No 334033 forms a service for Milngavie at Hyndland on 22 May 2019 *Bob Avery*

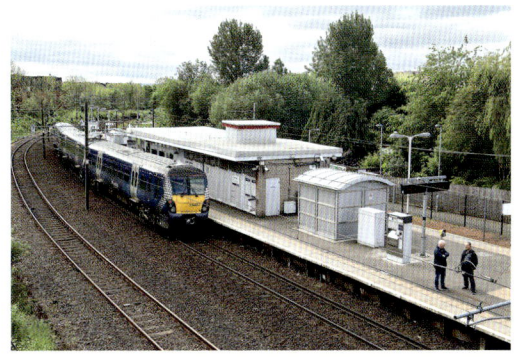

No 334037 leaves Hyndland with an eastbound service on the same day. *Bob Avery*

IBM		55 A1
Previous name	IBM Halt	
Opened	9 May 1978	
Closed	8 December 2018	
Operator	original BR	

The station, though a public one, was located in the middle of a large facility owned by IBM, a major employer in the area. However, IBM and other employers subsequently closed their premises and the station stood within a semi-derelict wasteland, attracting anti-social behaviour and little patronage, leading to its closure. At the time it was served by hourly trains to Glasgow and Wemyss Bay.

IBM station entrance, photographed on 10 June 2012. *Terry Gough*

Passengers Once More

A Glasgow to Wemyss Bay service formed of unit No 380111 pulls away from IBM station on the same day. This station closed in 2018. *Terry Gough*

Milliken Park		55 B2
Previous name	Cochrane Mill	
Opened	21 July 1840	
Closed	18 April 1966	
Reopened	15 May 1989	
Operator	*original* G&SWR	

A basic half-hourly service (with some extras at peak hours) operates between Glasgow and Ayr. In the evenings westbound trains run to Largs or Ardossan. On Sundays all westbound trains run to Ardrossan Harbour or Largs.

No 380110 calls at Milliken Park forming the 11.36 Ayr-Glasgow Central service on 25 March 2019. *Bob Avery*

Other Greater Glasgow stations

Ayrshire line services are monopolised by Class 380s, and two such units pass at Milliken Park, also on 25 March 2019. *Bob Avery*

Lochwinnoch		55 B2
Previous name	Lochside	
Opened	12 August 1840	
Closed	4 July 1955	
Reopened	27 June 1966	
Operator	original G&SWR	

Originally named Lochwinnoch, the name was changed to Lochside in 1905 when another Lochwinnoch station opened on the parallel Dalry to Johnstone line to the north. This newer station closed in 1966 and the original station reopened, reverting to the 'Lochwinnoch' name.

Above: The up (Glasgow-bound) platform is seen on the same day, showing the barely adequate parking facilities. *Bob Avery*

Left: Unit No 380011 arrives at Lochwinnoch as the 10.26 Ayr-Glasgow Central service on 29 April 2019. *Bob Avery*

Partick		103 B2
Opened	17 December 1979	
Operator	**original** BR	

Partick is Scotland's tenth busiest station. As well as serving Glasgow's West End residential and shopping areas and two major museums, it offers easy interchange with the city's circular Subway and several bus routes. The platforms of the former Partickhill station a short distance to the north-west, which Partick replaced, are visible from the platform ends. Almost all Argyle Line and North Electric services call here, offering a comprehensive and frequent train service.

Above right: Partick interchange, photographed on 22 May 2019, the date of all these pictures. The steps on the left lead to the rail platforms while the escalators on the right lead to the 4-foot-gauge Glasgow Subway. There are also bus connections outside. *Bob Avery*

Right and below right: No 334036, forming the 1154 Edinburgh-Helensburgh Central calls at Partick. In the second picture the down platform of the former Partick station can be clearly seen. *Both Bob Avery*

Other Greater Glasgow stations

No 334007, approaches Partick forms a westbound service for Dalmuir. *Bob Avery*

Priesthill & Darnley		103 C2
Opened	23 April 1990	
Operator	original BR	

A half-hourly weekday service between Glasgow Central and Barrhead calls here, as does an hourly Glasgow-Kilmarnock service on Sundays.

Below: No 156506 calls at Priesthill & Darnley as the 11.27 Glasgow Central-Barrhead service on 18 July 2019. *Bob Avery*

Above: Differential focus treatment is handed out to the 11.57 Barrhead-Glasgow Central service at Priesthill & Darnley on the same day. *Bob Avery*

Shieldmuir		56 B2
Opened	14 May 1990	
Operator	original BR	

Shieldmuir is located on the WCML south-east of Motherwell. Main-line trains do not call, but the station is served by half-hourly Argyle Line services to and from Lanark, with the odd peak-hour extra running to Carstairs instead. The station suffered from isolation, leading to vandalism and passenger intimidation prior to the introduction of CCTV. This latter, and nearby housing developments, have meant a gradual rise in patronage. The station is not far as the crow flies from the large Wishaw General Hospital, but the main entrance is a good 15-minute walk away. Shieldmuir Royal Mail Terminal, the starting point for daily mail trains to the south, is nearby.

GBRf's two Class 50 'Hoovers', Nos 50007 and 50048, pass Shieldmuir on a Motherwell to Scarborough excursion on 6 July 2019. *Bob Avery*

Stepps		104 B2
Previous name	Stepps Road	
Opened	May 1831	
Closed	5 November 1962	
Reopened	15 May 1989	
Operator	original CR	

The original Stepps Road station was a short distance to the east of the present one. A half-hourly electric Glasgow Queen Street to Edinburgh via Falkirk Grahamston and Cumbernauld service calls here, with an hourly Queen Street to Cumbernauld service on Sundays.

A Class 385 EMU accelerates away from Stepps on a Glasgow Queen Street to Edinburgh Waverley via Falkirk working on 30 March 2019. *Bob Avery*

Other Greater Glasgow stations

New Hitachi No 385110 calls at Stepps with a Glasgow Queen Street to Edinburgh via Cumbernauld and Falkirk Grahamston service, also on 30 March 2019. *Bob Avery*

Robroyston		(104 B1)
Opened	(1) c1899 (2) 1 June 1917	
Closed	(1) 1 January 1919 (2) 11 June 1956	
Reopened	15 December 2019	
Operator	*original* CR	

This is Scotland's newest station at the time of writing. Train services are as listed for Stepps.

Robroyston station under construction, 24 August 2019. *Bob Avery*

Above: No 385038 approaches Robroyston forming a Glasgow Queen Street-Falkirk Grahamston service on 11 September 2020, the date of these three views. *Bob Avery*

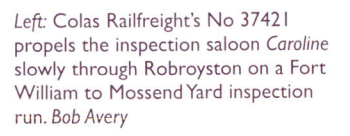

Left: Colas Railfreight's No 37421 propels the inspection saloon *Caroline* slowly through Robroyston on a Fort William to Mossend Yard inspection run. *Bob Avery*

No 385112 calls at Robroyston during its Falkirk Grahamston to Glasgow Queen Street run. *Bob Avery*

Other Greater Glasgow stations

Whifflet		56 C1
Opened	21 December 1992	
Operator	**original** BR	

This is a completely new station on a new site, though physically close to the sites of the former North British and bi-level Caledonian Railway stations, closed in September 1930 and November 1962 respectively. Initially the new station was served by an hourly diesel service between Motherwell and Cumbernauld. Following the introduction of passenger services over the line from Rutherglen East Junction (described elsewhere) in 2006, Whifflet became the terminus for a half-hourly service from Glasgow Central. Following electrification in 2014, both these services were incorporated into the Argyle Line service pattern. The little-used curve from Whifflet South Junction to Coatbridge Sunnyside Junction, which effectively links the north and south electric networks, bypasses the station. This curve was used by Lanark-Dalmuir services for seven months in 1995-96 during the Argyle Line's closure due to flood damage.

No 318254 arrives at Whifflet with a terminating service from Dalmuir on 16 July 2019. *Bob Avery*

Whinhill		55 A1
Opened	14 May 1990	
Operator	**original** BR	

This station is a completely new one on the Glasgow to Wemyss Bay line, serving the south side of the Clydeside town of Gourock. An hourly service operates in each direction.

Whinhill is seen looking towards Glasgow on 10 July 2012. The 310-yard-long Cartsburn Tunnel is at the end of the platform. *Terry Gough*

Shields Road (temporary station)		(103 B2)
Opened	12 December 1870	
Closed	14 February 1966	
Reopened	16 September 1978	
Operator	*original* G&SWR	

The original Shields Road was a complex station roughly on the site of what is now the busy Shields Junction, where the original line to Glasgow St Enoch and the new line to Glasgow Central split. The name was resurrected for a temporary platform within Shields Maintenance Depot to allow shuttles from Glasgow Central to bring visitors to an open day there in 1978. (It is not to be confused with Shields Road station on the Glasgow Underground Railway.)

Greater Glasgow lines

Gartsherrie South Junction to Garnqueen North Junction (Coatbridge Central to Greenfaulds)	56 C1

This short stretch has no stations but regained regular services in 1996 with the introduction of a Motherwell to Cumbernauld service. Since then it has gained a frequent service with the extension of electrification, and has become part of the Argyle Line timetable. Before that summer Motorail trains to Stirling (until 1989) and the Euston-Inverness 'Clansman' provided a passenger service, though the 'Clansman' was later rerouted to run via Edinburgh.

Cowlairs South Junction to Sighthill West Junction (Cowlairs Chord Line)	104 B1

This sharply curved single-track route opened in 1993 and provided a long overdue direct line from Springburn into Glasgow Queen Street station. Prior to that most trains from Cumbernauld terminated at Springburn and city-bound travellers had to change to an EMU service via Bellgrove to Queen Street Low Level. Some later ran through, involving reversal at Cowlairs West Junction. The new curve creates a triangle of lines, in the centre of which are Network Rail offices, including the Regional Control Office and the West of Scotland signalling centre.

Mother Nature is trying hard to reclaim the sharply curved Cowlairs Chord Line as No 385106 squeals around as the 10.55 Glasgow Queen Street to Edinburgh via Falkirk Grahamston working on 30 July 2019. *Bob Avery*

Other Greater Glasgow stations

Forming a triangle at the top of Glasgow's Cowlairs Incline (on the line out of Queen Street) – top left of picture – the Cowlairs Chord Line allows trains to run directly to Springburn, and No 385106 is doing exactly that. The triangle contains various Network Rail offices. Bob Avery

Cumbernauld to Greenhill Lower Junction — 56 A1

The line north of Cumbernauld saw little passenger use apart from the daily 'Clansman' and summer Motorail services. But in 1999 regular services between Glasgow and Falkirk Grahamston were introduced, and these trains are now part of a fully electrified half-hourly service from Glasgow to Edinburgh via Falkirk Grahamston.

Holytown Junction to Wishaw — 56 B1

This stretch of line was electrified with the Anglo-Scottish WCML electrification in 1974, to allow electrically hauled freight services access to and from Mossend Yard and Coatbridge Freightliner terminal without passing through the already congested Motherwell station. It passed very close to the former Ravenscraig steelworks and offered excellent views of the ore and coal unloading facilities. It acquired a passenger service in 2007 with the routing of one tph each way from Lanark to Dalmuir via this rather circuitous routing, approaching Motherwell from the north, then proceeding via Hamilton. Alternate Lanark trains took the more straightforward route via Wishaw, Shieldmuir, Motherwell and Bellshill. In 2017 all Lanark trains reverted to running via Bellshill and were diverted into Glasgow Central main high-level station. Today one peak-hour train each way from Carstairs runs this way, and also a handful of Virgin 'Pendolino' services to and from London Euston. There have been suggestions that trains that currently terminate at Whifflet might be extended over this route to Wishaw, as some run empty to Wishaw to turn anyway.

AYRSHIRE STATIONS

Ardrossan Town		55 B1
Previous name	Ardrossan	
Opened	1831	
Closed	1 January 1968	
Reopened	19 January 1987	
Operator	original G&SWR	

One of three stations in this Ayrshire coast town, it was originally a terminus, but became a through station when the line was extended to Ardrossan Harbour in 1850. Renaming to Ardrossan Town occurred on 2 March 1953. During its closure period it was used to stable DMUs.

Taken from the ruins of Ardrossan Castle, unit No 380111 waits to take the short run down to Ardrossan Harbour station on 9 June 2012. *Terry Gough*

Viewed on the same day, beyond the single-platform Ardrossan Town station are the remains of the 15th-century Ardrossan Castle. The open level crossing (since modified with full barriers) takes the Harbour Branch across Arran Place. 9 June 2012. *Terry Gough*

Ayrshire stations

Kilmaurs		55 C2
Opened	26 June 1873	
Closed	7 November 1966	
Reopened	12 May 1984	
Operator	original GB&KR	

A basically half-hourly (hourly on Sundays) service operates each way between Glasgow Central and Kilmarnock, with selected trains going forward to either Carlisle or Stranraer. The pre-closure station building (replacing the original, which burned down in 1914) was reported to be the only one in Scotland with central heating!

A Glasgow Central-bound Class 156 unit runs into the single platform at Kilmaurs on 9 June 2012. *Terry Gough*

Stewarton		55 B2
Opened	27 March 1871	
Closed	7 November 1966	
Reopened	5 June 1967	
Operator	original GB&KR	

This is another new station on the now busy Glasgow to Kilmarnock corridor, short-sightedly singled in the 1970s. Stewarton achieved unwelcome attention on 27 January 2009 when, during work to redouble a portion of the route, a road bridge collapsed as a loaded oil train was passing over it, causing derailment and fire, fortunately without injury. Train services are similar to those for Kilmaurs.

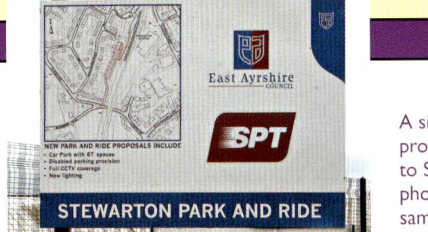

A sign giving details of proposed improvements to Stewarton station, photographed on the same day. *Terry Gough*

A Glasgow-bound Class 156 unit, which will probably have originated in Kilmarnock, arrives at Stewarton on 9 June 2012. *Terry Gough*

Dunlop		55 B2
Opened	27 March 1871	
Closed	7 November 1966	
Reopened	8 June 1967	
Operator	original GB&KR	

Like its neighbour Stewarton, this station's period of closure after Beeching was brief thanks to vigorous local campaigning. It acquired a second platform after part of the route was redoubled in 2009. Train services are as those listed for Kilmaurs.

Right: Bunting signals the approach of the community gala day – a common local event in the greater Glasgow area – at Dunlop station on 9 June 2012. *Terry Gough*

No 156435 on a Glasgow Central-Barrhead-Kilmarnock working pauses at Dunlop, also on 9 June 2012. *Terry Gough*

Ayrshire stations

Prestwick International Airport		55 C2
Previous name	Glasgow Prestwick Airport	
Opened	5 September 1994	
Operator	**original** Glasgow Prestwick Airport (train operator: BR)	

This station offers easy transfer to the airport by means of a covered elevated walkway. It enjoys four tph in each direction between Glasgow Central and Ayr (two tph on Sundays). It is unique in that it is managed by the airport authority rather than ScotRail (which of course operates the trains). Despite its superb rail links to the city, Prestwick Airport has lost out to Glasgow and Edinburgh airports in terms of destinations served.

Prestwick Airport station is seen looking towards Glasgow on 9 June 2012. The footbridge continues right over the adjacent main road and leads directly to the terminal building. *Terry Gough*

Auchinleck		55 C2
Opened	9 August 1848	
Closed	6 December 1965	
Reopened	12 May 1984	
Operator	**original** G&SWR	

Located on the G&SWR Carlisle to Glasgow secondary route, the station also serves the neighbouring and slightly larger town of Cumnock, through which the railway passes but has no station. Reopening was probably prompted by an attempt to revitalise the local economy, depleted by colliery closures. There are 11 trains each way (though one southbound service only goes as far as neighbouring New Cumnock). Occasional trains go beyond Carlisle to Newcastle. There are a meagre two trains each way on Sundays.

No 156478 draws into Auchinleck on 9 June 2012, where a number of passengers heading south will board. *Terry Gough*

No 156478 accelerates away from Auchinleck on its journey to Carlisle over the former G&SWR main line. Terry Gough

New Cumnock		51 A1
Opened	20 May 1850	
Closed	6 December 1965	
Reopened	27 May 1991	
P&P	No 19 p57	
Operator	**original** G&SWR	

This original G&SWR station reopened to serve the town of the same name, and train services are as shown for Auchinleck. The station building survives as NR's Permanent Way offices. The town was at the centre of Ayrshire opencast coal-mining renaissance, and is close to the former colliery at Knockshinnoch, location of a mining disaster in 1950 that claimed 13 lives. Also nearby is the newer branch to Greenburn opencast, and a coal-loading area adjacent to the station itself. All have fallen into disuse in recent years as coal has fallen out of favour as a fuel for power generation.

No 66026 heads south through New Cumnock on 8 August 2005 with another load of Ayrshire coal in older HAA-type vehicles. In the background No 66037 is in the loading area with modern HTA wagons. The Ayrshire coal boom was at its height, though such traffic on the G&SWR line has since dwindled from teens of trains each day to just three per week in 2019. Bob Avery

Ayrshire stations 125

New Cumnock's down-side station buildings are now in use as Network Rail's local Permanent Way offices. *Terry Gough*

Barassie to Kilmarnock Line

This stretch of line has no intermediate stations, but is one of Scotland's oldest lines and owes its existence to coal traffic. It acquired a limited service in 1975 – and the daily and overnight Euston-Stranraer trains – but more recently a reasonable service between Kilmarnock, Ayr, Girvan and Stranraer has been introduced.

This is Cockhill (no station) on the single line between Barassie and Kilmarnock, with Goat Fell on the Isle of Arran in the background. On 18 April 1995 Nos 37358 and 37350 have charge of the 11.35 Falkland-Blyth Power Station service, with coal from Killoch washery. Needless to say this location is now completely overgrown. *Bob Avery*

DUMFRIES & GALLOWAY STATIONS

Sanquhar		51 A1
Opened	28 October 1850	
Closed	6 December 1965	
Reopened	27 June 1994	
Operator	original G&SWR	

This is another reopened station on the G&SWR route to serve the town and the surrounding countryside. Train services are as shown for Auchinleck.

This view of Sanquhar, looking towards Glasgow, shows the attractive G&SWR station buildings. *Terry Gough*

Looking in the opposite direction towards Carlisle on the same day, 9 June 2012. *Terry Gough* It's a damp day with skies that

Gretna Green		52 C1
Previous name	Gretna	
Opened	23 August 1848	
Closed	6 December 1965	
Reopened	20 September 1993	
P&P	No 19 p42	
Operator	original G&SWR	

The station was reopened to serve the town of Gretna and the village of Gretna Green, famous for its facilities for arranging weddings! Originally reopened with a single platform, a second platform was added in 2008 when the G&SWR route was redoubled to accommodate booming coal traffic, which has sadly now virtually ceased. The NBR also had a station at Gretna, shut as long ago as 1915, on a short branch from Langholm on its 'Waverley Route'. Train services are as shown for Auchinleck, with the addition of extra trains to and from Dumfries only, giving a basic hourly service as far as Dumfries.

threaten more to come as Freightliner's No 66522 heads north through Gretna Green with coal empties on 8 June 2012. *Terry Gough*

INDEX OF LOCATIONS

H = Heritage or tourist railway; T = Temporary station

Airbles 101
Alloa 45
Alness 9
Anderston 80
Ardrossan Town 120
Argyle Street 82
Armadale 55
Ashfield 94
Auchinleck 123
Aviemore Speyside (H) 19
Baillieston 92
Balmossie 36
Barassie to Kilmarnock line 125
Bargeddie 92
Bathgate 54
Beauly 10
Birkhill (H) 78
Blackridge 56
Bo'ness (H) 76
Boat of Garten (H) 21
Branchton 102
Brechin (H) 33
Bridge of Allan 46
Bridge of Dun (H) 35
Bridgeton 83
Broomhill (H) 22
Brunstane 59
Caldercruix 57
Camelon 47
Carmyle 90
Chatelherault 98
Conon Bridge 12
Corkerhill 89
Cowlairs Chord Line 118
Crookston 87
Culross (T) 43
Cumbernauld to Greenhill Lower Junction line 119
Curriehill 67
Dalgety Bay 40
Dalmarnock 84
Drumfrochar 103
Drumgelloch 58
Drummuir (H) 24
Drumry 104
Dufftown (H) 23

Dumbreck 90
Duncraig 13
Dunfermline Queen Margaret 41
Dunlop 122
Dunrobin Castle 14
Dyce 27
Edinburgh Gateway 69
Edinburgh Park 51
Eskbank 2, 61
Exhibition Centre 81
Falls of Cruachan 49
Galashiels 65
Garscadden 105
Gartcosh 106
Gartsherrie South Junction to Garnqueen North Junction line 118
Gilshochill 95
Glasgow Central Low Level 82
Glenrothes with Thornton 42
Golf Street 38
Gorebridge 63
Greenfaulds 107
Gretna Green 127
Hawkhead 87
Holytown Junction to Wishaw line 119
Howwood 108
Hyndland 109
IBM 109
Invergarry (H) 18
Keith Town (H) 26
Kelvindale 97
Kilmaurs 121
Kingsknowe 70
Kinneil (H) 78
Kintore 28
Kirkwood 93
Larkhall 99
Laurencekirk 30
Livingston North 53
Livingston South 71
Loch Awe 48
Loch Eil Outward Bound 50
Lochluichart 14
Lochwinnoch 111
Manuel (H) 79
Maryhill 96

Meadowbank 75
Merryton 99
Milliken Park 110
Milton of Crathes (H) 32
Mosspark 88
Mount Vernon 91
Muir of Ord 16
Musselburgh 73
New Cumnock 124
Newcraighall 60
Newtongrange 62
Paisley Canal 86
Partick 112
Perth to Ladybank line 44
Portlethen 29
Possilpark & Parkhouse 95
Prestwick International Airport 123
Priesthill & Darnley 113
Robroyston 115
Rogart 17
Rutherglen 85
Sanquhar 126
Shawfair 61
Shieldmuir 114
Shields Road (T) 118
South Gyle 68
Stepps 114
Stewarton 121
Stow 64
Summerston 96
Towiemore (H) 25
Tweedbank 66
Uphall 52
Wallyford 74
Wester Hailes 72
Whifflet 117
Whinhill 117
Winchburgh Jn to Dalmeny line 76